Janez Juhant, Bojan Žalec (Eds.)

Understanding Genocide and Suicide

Theologie Ost – West

Europäische Perspektiven

herausgegeben von

Prof. Dr. Janez Juhant
(Universität Ljubljana)
und Prof. Dr. Albert Franz
(Universität Dresden)

Band 18

LIT

Understanding Genocide and Suicide

edited by

Janez Juhant and Bojan Žalec

LIT

Cover image: Alenka Doblekar, Photomontage

This book is printed on acid-free paper.

Bibliographic information published by the Deutsche Nationalbibliothek
The Deutsche Nationalbibliothek lists this publication in the Deutsche Nationalbibliografie; detailed bibliographic data are available in the Internet at http://dnb.d-nb.de.

ISBN 978-3-643-90527-7

A catalogue record for this book is available from the British Library

Klosbachstr. 107
CH-8032 Zürich
Tel. +41 (0) 44-251 75 05 Fax +41 (0) 44-251 75 06
E-Mail: zuerich@lit-verlag.ch http://www.lit-verlag.ch
Distribution:
In the UK: Global Book Marketing, e-mail: mo@centralbooks.com
In North America: International Specialized Book Services, e-mail: orders@isbs.com
In Germany: LIT Verlag Fresnostr. 2, D-48159 Münster
Tel. +49 (0) 2 51-620 32 22, Fax +49 (0) 2 51-922 60 99, E-mail: vertrieb@lit-verlag.de
In Austria: Medienlogistik Pichler-ÖBZ, e-mail: mlo@medien-logistik.at
e-books are available at www.litwebshop.de

Acknowledgments

We thank to all persons who have contributed to the appearing of the book. Our special thanks go to: the reviewers – professor Ciril Sorč from the Faculty of Theology and professor Matjaž Potrč from the Faculty of Arts, both University of Ljubljana; to Valerija Japelj for proofreading and corrections of the manuscript; to Vojko Strahovnik for the layout and help by editing of the manuscript; and last but not least, to all the authors of the book.

This book was prepared and published with the support of Slovenian Research Agency (ARRS) founded research programme P6-0269 (A) Ethical and religious foundation and perspectives of society and religiology in context of modern education.

Janez Juhant and Bojan Žalec, the editors

Ljubljana, December 2014

CONTENTS

INTRODUCTION

Proper understanding, defining and evaluation of genocide and suicide, their kinds, factors and conditions, scientific deepening and historical and cultural-comparative researches are crucial in order to be more successful in future by their prevention and timely recognition. Therefore we should consider every scientific contribution to them as very precious. In this book genocide and suicide are considered from several scientific points of view: theological, religiological, philosophical, historical, sociological, educational, psycho therapeutical and legal. The book contains eighteen essays divided in three chapters. The following main topics and theses are considered in them.

Foundations: anthropological, philosophical and conceptual clarifications

Juhant highlights the connectedness of suicide and genocide with the phenomena of depersonalisation of man and society, and the development of science and technics in modernity as crucial factors of the genocidal phenomena of 20th century. **Žalec's** essay brings a survey of factors and indicators of genocide as they are revealed by several scientific disciplines (psychology, cultural anthropology, science of politics etc.) and by multidisciplinary approach. This knowledge is very important since without it no other part of the picture of genocide (its conceptual analysis and definition, its discerning from the similar phenomena (mass murders, crime against humanity etc.), strategies to prevent or to decrease the chances of it, coping with its consequences etc.) can be provided in a grounded, verified and an efficient way. **Klun** presents Kierkegaardian view on suicide. He compares it with Heidegger's one and considers it as a fruitful basis of a deeper approach to suicide. **Petkovšek** deals with violence - including suicide and genocide - in the frame of Girard's mimetic theory. The way out from the mimetic circle (of violence) is to obey the will of God (by following Christ's example). **Strahovnik** analyses the concept of genocide by means of different concepts of harm (done to a group), and concludes "with some ideas about a more suitable definition and understanding of the concept of genocide that would reach beyond its established delineation in international law". **Letnar Černič** discusses different definitions of genocide, also in the light of judiciary practice and points out some of the limits of these definitions.

Historical, sociological, religiological and theological dimensions

Méster indicates how the specific sentiment after the WW I triggered the philosophical discussions on the topic of suicide. The core of the article is to show how the broader view of the philosopher J. Posch - a prominent cultural person of Hungary - determined his interpretation of suicide. At the end Mester shows the impact of Posch's approach to suicide on broader discussion on this topic in Hungary. The controversy between Posch and Milán Füst is analysed. **Kovács** presents István Bibó's explanation of the holocaust in Hungary. **Griesser- Pečar** –

by way of presenting the mass killings in Slovenia after the WW II - tries to contribute to the proper answer to the question whether the intentional killing of the members of a particular political group should be considered as a form of genocide. **Kačerauskas** deals with the issue of suicide in the contexts of cultural industry and creativity. He claims that suicide can be interpreted as a revolt of an individual against his (her) controlling from the side of society. **Smoczynski** - in his sociological paper - deals with the role of religious organizations in constraining the possibility of committing suicide. He concludes that "according to the growing amount of gathered data on the relationship between religion and suicide risk it seems that this is the mutual reinforcing effect of religious normative aspect and tangible networking that reduces suicide expectancy among religionists". **Osredkar's** main thesis is that individualism - which manifests itself on the religious area as secularization - leads to the death of European civilization. In this context he deals with the (theological) reasons for the lacking basis for human rights in the contemporary Western society. **Prijatelj** claims that narcissism is the first consequence of the solitarist view on human identity. She distinguishes two fundamental types of suicide: a metamorphic suicide and an executive suicide. She tries to find a possible way in order to avoid terrible consequences of monolith identity. The path to overcome the crisis of identity is moral imagination in which "many common identities will be recognized and mutual differences will be respected". The paper surveys and summarizes the current state of understanding on the topic (Sen, Ronningstam, Lederach,Taylor and others) but it brings a new syntheses which also includes the author's own observations (e.g. about Slovenians and their mental condition).

Education, personal formation, therapy and law

Gerjolj's paper belongs to the area of educational science. He shows how the Bible (in particular the story of Moses) can help us by education for life which however is an important factor in combating suicide. **Erzar & Erzar** consider - from the psycho-therapeutic point of view - the complex phenomenon of playing the victim in the cycle of violence at the individual as well at the group level. They disclose the connection of the dynamic playing of a victim with experiences in the past violent and abusive social regimes. The topic of **Godawa's** paper is a martyr's preparation for death. On the basis of St. Thomas More's writing he presents its structure and concludes: "According to the aim of theology of spirituality, which is a description of spiritual experience, the scheme showed here may serve as a point of references in further research as well as in forming one's personal life not only facing a direct perspective of death but also in 'everyday little martyrdom' where love still turns out to be stronger than sinful death." **Slatinek** illuminates the important connection between suicide and hopelessness. His reflection is grounded on the evidence from the Rotae Romanae tribunal cases. **Strehovec** analyzes the importance of family for personal and societal formation.

Janez Juhant and Bojan Žalec, the editors

SUICIDE AND GENOCIDE IN THE CONTEXT OF MODERNITY

Janez Juhant, *Ljubljana*

The article is divided into three parts. The first part deals with the societal conditions of modernity which were radically changed in the new ages by the development of science and technics. In the second part I discuss problems of suicide and genocide in those conditions. The third part deals with attempts to asses those complex problems of modernity.

Part I

Introduction

The society of modernity has come to labyrinths, because of person's desire to regulate her life and her inability to manage it. This is the cause of the disorder and sideways, which radically shook the human grounds, commenced self-confidence in person's capabilities and opened the problem of human self-regulation. This remains a problem in the present times and raises the question of human balance (self/world) and related to that the questions of the meaning of human life and the survival of human kind.

Eugen Biser (1995, 267) states: "In the context of today's world, *conditio humana* (condition of human life) appears ambiguous: as a burden and as encouraging. Encouraging because, out of this conditions go initiatives, which consolidate human being in setting free his inexplicated capabilities and to transcendent status of his actual being in the acts of persistent making better of himself. But on the other hand he is actually burdened with complex of directive powers, which are turning himself from his own personality. This inflicts above all the basic human hope".

Concerning first part of this quotation the human life today is open towards new possibilities and in connection with this also insured with new discoveries in modern medical and retirement fund systems and other inventions. People, living in developed societies, are used to live on tracks, in fixed conditions, being provided for by science and technics. We rely on such various insurances, which should provide for us care in sickness and old age; we create controlled living conditions, in which we are supposed to live as comfortable as we can. We enhance our world with medical assistance, internet, radio, television … Our common day seems to be logical, complete, structured and arranged, with no deficiencies. In short, an individual should live in a designed framework, and this framework completely defines the life of individuals and communities alike.

These new discoveries and benefits in the modern era also brought disorders and sideways that radically shook fundamentals of human being, emerged doubts in humans and their abilities and opened a problem of human self-organizing, which still affects humankind. Consequences are troubles of balance toward the self and the outside world, also opening the question about purpose of human life and survival of humankind.

What does this mean? Vasily Grossman, a Russian Jew, pointed out in the novel *Life and Fate* that the time of totalitarianisms produces a strong feeling of fatalism like in "Hitlerism" and Bolshevism. This concerns a basic change of human and lack of feeling in his/her own personality and character and related to this "the feeling of fatefulness was increasing." (Grossman 1995, 204) The hero of the book, Jewish physician Sofja Osipovna "was wondering by herself that just some days were necessary to come to reverse way from human to the dirty and unhappy nameless livestock, plundered freedom, meanwhile the way to the human was going millions of years"(206).

Exclusion of others

The violent educational and political oppression against religious views shaped individual and societal consciousness, establishing a militant atheistic ideology, building an atheistic society, excluding others as different. This endures as a burden in post-communist and other post-totalitarian countries. The phenomenon of a systematic and violent "atheisation" without free individual and societal ways for individuals and the whole society in (post)totalitarian times remains.

This new "ideology of success dominates" (Girard 1989, 157) and the remnants of rivalry and exclusion of class-enemies have become a custom. Still Girard argues that Christianity has significantly contributed to the real picture of victimisation and victims, but many modern authors didn't want to realize this (Girard 2001, chap. XIII). "In the future, all violence will reveal what Christ's Passion revealed, the foolish genesis of blood-stained idols and false gods of religion, politics, and ideologies." (Girard 1989, 212) Nazism attempted to absolve Germany and then the whole of Europe from caring for the victims (Girard 2001, chap. XIV); the same can be said of Marxism. The exclusion of religion via accusation and establishing of violence is a "*proprium*" of modern ideologies which reaches its full realization in the totalitarian systems. The consequence of this "bad conscience" was burdening of religions with predictive "violence", to diminish one's own violence, to provide an excuse, to "kill" the religious tradition of brotherhood of all people and to change societies by violent revolutionary methods. This has had fatal consequences in the Balkans and in the wars of former Yugoslavia.

Exclusion of religious-spiritual heritage

Today we are facing a new challenge, a new moment in modern civilization, which Jacques Monod (1990, 281) describes "as rejection of centuries old spiritual tradition where spirituality is a decisive source of knowledge". The separation of politics and other spheres of societal life from religion is a complex process. The enlightenment project needs to be completed by addressing an important anthropological dimension of each person – the spiritual one (Wallach 2011). The lack of a religious-spiritual dimension caused wars in post-communist and other countries of different transitions, because people had no ethical grounds to challenge the otherness but only posed the borders to the other, viewing the other as a (class) enemy. The Enlightenment's ideologies especially in their violent communist forms opened struggles against religion, as Casanova (1994, 24) states: "However, as the Newtonian Enlightenment crossed the Channel, it became patently radicalized and militantly antireligious. Science was transformed into a scientific and scientist worldview which claimed to have replaced religion in the same way a new scientific paradigm replaces an outmoded one".

Gianni Vattimo (1997) asserts that Christianity played an important role regarding the origins of modern socio-cultural heritage. But the Enlightenment's attempt was to establish an autonomous anthropological or societal concept of "just", "moral" (Kant 1956), or modern "neutral" civil religion, in which God is an "empty sign" (Bellah 1991). We can find signs of this distinction in works of many thinkers. Beginning with Locke (1955, 17; cf. Cavanaugh 2009, 80), as Ezra Kopelowitz (2003, 86-87) mentions, and after Locke "the religious-secular binary is a new creation that accompanies the creation of the modern state". Kopelowitz adds that the "distinction between the 'religious' and the 'secular' occurs in societies in which the individual rather than (the) group is the primary component of social organization" (ibid.). Individual persons were the ground of the modern state and religion was thus considered to be a personal matter, and not a state issue. However this development causes dualism between the societal and the individual sphere or a kind of schizophrenia. On the one side the individual has his "own" religion; on the other he belongs to the national, political and to the religious community. The Marxists and other totalitarianisms benefited from this to subordinate the person under the totalitarian order. In particular the Catholic and other Churches trained their believers in obedience to make them available for their tasks. Religion was considered as a "private matter" but at the same time politics was trying to find a common (a-theistic) ideological ground or to span religious elements in state affairs. Casanova (1994, 21) locates four reasons for this modern development: "the Protestant Reformation; the formation of modern states, the growth of modern capitalism, and early modern scientific revolution". The last one was used as a parade horse of Marxism. All implied the new organisation of modern societies with individualisation and search for the new ideological, non-religious grounds on which the society will be founded. This was not always the path toward subsidiarity but rather toward ideologization or totalitarization in the totalitarian systems, which remains an anthropological problem of former Marxist societies, because Marxist ideology seriously injured human nature.

In the very beginning of this development was the question of the role of religion in (modern) society. At the same time the struggle between the religious sphere on the one hand and the civil, so called "a-theistic" sphere on the other culminated in societal battles of the Modern Era. This was evident particularly in the 20th century as the totalitarian regimes took total possession over the societal sphere, including religion. These "conversions" were accompanied by big societal disturbances, struggles, and wars (Alexander 1987; Pipes 1995; Snyder 2012). A private, individual religious sphere as a basis of the modernity was usually violently "integrated" by the so-called "a-theistic ideologies" or worldviews.

In modernity the experiences of religion were marked by many ideological and political dimensions, which were fixed by liberal: freemason (Alexander 1987, 30), socialist or so called civil, humanistic, "neutral", or non-liturgical (Hobsbawm 1983; Cavanaugh 2009, 113) worldview of man. Modern understanding of religion contained more political than religious connotations. Religion was expanded in the socio-political and strategic circumstances of modern development as was the case with the religions in Bosnia and Herzegovina: "The traditional religion is privatized, while the religion of politics occupies the public realm" (Cavanaugh 2009, 116).

The myth of religious violence

"For its many avid consumers in the West, the myth of religious violence serves on the domestic scene to marginalize discourses and practices labelled religious, especially those associated with Christian churches, particularly in Europe, with Muslim groups. The myth helps to reinforce adherence to a secular social order and the nation-state that guarantees it. … The myth of religious violence is also useful, therefore, for justifying secular violence against religious actors; their irrational violence must be met with rational violence. … The myth of religious violence should finally be seen for what it is: an important part of the folklore of Western societies. It does not identify any facts about the world, but rather authorizes certain arrangements of power in the modern West. It is a story of salvation from mortal peril by the creation of a secular national state." (Cavanaugh 2009, 225-6) Tony Judt's (Judt, Snyder 2012, 98ff.) analysis of the European history is a good example of the missing role of intellectuals with critical relations to the political power. To conclude this part: the modern society is a transition society, changing for centuries valid norms and habits, in case of Marxist regimes also the inherent anthropological values. The space of human was opened, undefined, and challenging for its societal capabilities. The liberal society doesn't secure the conditions in which it lives (Böckenförde 1976). These conditions influence both the phenomena of suicide and genocide, thus we will proceed with some observations on them, which will expose their psychological and societal conditions and reveal that the problem arises with conditions of life in modernity, highlighting the ways to prevent them.

Part II

Suicide

"Suicide is an act with which someone intentionally causes his own death" (SSKJ IV, 377), "he executes himself" (Milčinski 1986, 11). Concerning Milčinski, somatic part has a crucial role in suicide (17); in opposition to that Durkheim (1992) emphasizes societal reasons for suicide. Milčinski searches for reasons for suicide also in physical and mental conditions of individual. Trstenjak claims that suicide "depends on our inner dispositions, we could say on personal structure" (Trstenjak 1988, 576), which is not just personal or family determined, but also a question of (Western) civilization, or as Lev Šestov (2002, 113) wrote: "Our century is labelled as century of nihilism *par excellence*".

Suicide is a very complex individual and societal phenomenon, but societal conditions are very influential for it (Durkheim 1992/1887). As sociologists, Durkheim emphasizes the cultural or social role of suicide. Fritz Riemann (1998, 15) also sees connections between different types of humans through genetic determinations and early development of human personality. Suicides are more common among men what confirms that women are "strongest" gender. Durkheim establishes that suicide is more common among Protestants, less common among Catholics, and even less common among Jews.

Durkheim (1992, 69-72) distinguishes between three different types of suicide.

1. Egoistic suicide concerns a personality who is concerned only about himself and of his own ego. This psychological type is similar to Riemann's emphasis on fear of losing himself and inability to connect with other.
2. Altruistic suicide concerns a personality who is completely turned out of himself, towards others, towards society. This reveals the second type of fear, which concerns preserving oneself, but because of extroverted personality this can lead to giving oneself for others, instead of growing up and becoming independent. Such suicides are and were for example Japanese kamikaze and Islamic terrorists, who were prepared to give their own lives for their community (Riemann 1998, 199).
3. Anomic type, which means lacking norms and emerges when in the society values are no more accepted in the same sense as before and so-

> cietal changes go so far to establish a valueless system in which individual feels uncompleted and empty. Such a situation we find in societies of modernity and it is also a reason for the growing number of suicides. It is also a very serious problem of transition in several post-communist countries too.

Durkheim (1992, 31) is pointing out two different, antagonistic forces: “The first one results from community and wants to incorporate individual; the second one comes from individual and denies the first one.” Despite social status being formally regulated, the problem of weak relationships between people remains. This is the cause that suicide is correlated with difficulties of social relations of individuals, beside psychological reasons and mental diseases. We may conclude that community is crucial for preventing suicide.

Genocide

The *Declaration UN on Human Rights* in the Preamble specifies grounds for the prevention of violation of human rights: “Whereas recognition of the inherent dignity and of the equal and inalienable rights of all members of the human family is the foundation of freedom, justice and peace in the world, whereas disregard and contempt for human rights have resulted in barbarous acts which have outraged the conscience of mankind, and the advent of a world in which human beings shall enjoy freedom of speech and belief and freedom from fear and want has been proclaimed as the highest aspiration of the common people, whereas it is essential, if man is not to be compelled to have recourse, as a last resort, to rebellion against tyranny and oppression, that human rights should be protected by the rule of law …” (Preamble)

The convention on genocide prepared on 9th December 1948 and proclaimed on 12th January 1951 provides a definition and enumerates following “types” of genocide. Genocide “means any of the following acts committed with intent to destroy, in whole or in part, a national, ethnical, racial or religious group, as such: (a) Killing members of the group; (b) Causing serious bodily or mental harm to members of the group; (c) Deliberately inflicting on the group conditions of life calculated to bring about its physical destruction in whole or in part; (d) Imposing measures intended to prevent births within the group; (e) Forcibly transferring children of the group to another group.”

History of the 20th century is covered with genocidal blood, beginning genocide against Armenians in 1915, Ukrainians in the communist Soviet Union in 1932-33, Jews in Germans concentration camps, and followed by killings of the opponents of the communism in Yugoslavia and elsewhere, mass murders in 1994 of Tutsis in Ruanda, caused by Hutu's extremists, genocide over Muslims in BIH, especially in Srebrenica in July 1995. Genocide remains a problem and opens questions about asserting principles, by which we could sanction such incidents of inhumanity and against humanity, particularly in view of the ones responsible (usually connected with authorities) that do not confess their involvement in crimes, for example in the Slovenian communism. Neither Resolution 1481 of Parliamentary Assembly of the Council of Europe (PACE), published on 25the January 2006, on Condemnation of communism, fascism and Nazism, nor Resolution of Parliamentary Assembly of the Council of Europe (PACE), published on 2nd April 2009, on *European consciousness and totalitarianism* were accepted as our own (Slovenian). And that is why neither anniversary of the Slovene Partisan's battle in Dražgoše against Germans, nor anniversary of mass killing in Huda jama (Death cave), for us are not (yet) anniversaries of the memory of the victims, but sadly still opportunities for false, common political confrontations not worthy of humans. Similarly the August 23rd as the European day of Remembrance for victims of all totalitarianisms does not have national-state based grounds.

Modernity and Relationships: Exclusionist Competitiveness

Suicide and genocide are signs of a diseased condition of humans or humankind. Both designate difficult conditions of humankind of modernity and both are consequences of the impairment of fundamental human essence. Specific impairments can be experienced by those nations which have already suffered from some totalitarian system.

Trstenjak differentiates between three different types of nations and individuals. Introverted personalities, like Slovenes, are more offensive against themselves and more prone to suicide than other nations, for example Albanians and the nations of the South of Europe. In the modern society there are more reasons for aggression and it is more prone to genocide and aggression against others. Trstenjak says: "… according to intra- and extraversion a human being can be more aggressive to himself or others." (575) That shows the influence of social condition on both, individuals and nations, as reasons for suicide or genocide. Similarly, Eugen Biser (1995, 287) talks about "collective hospitalization" which is created by the circumstances of terror and subjection in totalitarian systems.

According to researches of Arendt, Bauman, Snyder, and others, we may say that modern society almost forces a human being into aggression, and that is why suicide, as Trstenjak claims, is a phenomenon of the Western society and its modern achievements, and less of the Eastern society, which is more or fully spiritual, but this is changing now. The main reason – according to Trstenjak – for lower rate of suicides in the East lies in the primal way of living; the reason behind higher rate in the West is artificiality of life. But there could also be a deeper cause: in the West, there are no sincere relationships. Suicide rate increases in the periods of crisis of individuals (puberty, climacteric) and society (unemployment).

Suicide and genocide lead to (dis)trust. "Hope is not conviction that something would turn out good, but certainty, that something has its meaning, no matter how it turns out eventually" (Havel 2012, 11). That is why neither suicide nor genocide, in anthropological sense, is at the end. As prisoners in concentration camps (CC) claim (Pahor 2008), there were no or few occasions of suicide or just thinking about it in camps, even though there was no escape given the genocidal plan. The victims of CC were full of hope and believed that one day they would regain their humanity. Trstenjak concludes: "Despair is the strongest and the most convincing proof that human is a hopeful being. By the time he loses this hope, his existence converses to its opposite, when he cannot live anymore. Desperation is a psychological fundament and predecessor of suicide: desperation is the only right reason why someone commits suicide, no matter direct cause and circumstances in which suicide was committed. To lose hope means to lose the meaning of life and power to strengthen the life. Both are connected. When someone loses (or cannot find) the meaning of his life, he/she does not have any reason to live forward, he/she does not have strength to live, and this is the state of despair" (Trstenjak 1988, 100). People living in the West are more susceptible to suicide because they are afraid of suffering, which is confirmed with research on euthanasia. Older persons are inclined to accept it, out of fear of loneliness and suffering. The younger want to be free of the older who are a burden for them. Sometimes the last is also the reason accepted by the older. Suicides are rarer in the countries with lower living standard.

Similarly genocide is a phenomenon of the modern society which eradicates traditional values. Suicide and genocide are based on impersonal, systematic and operative criteria of leading civilization.

That is why Trstenjak (1988, 582) presupposes ordered circumstances in order to prevent suicides. The first factor is psychological stability. The second is a capability to take a transcendent perspective in ordinary or everyday situations and relationships. Such capability Trstenjak explains as personal faith or transcendent posture. For both an exercise is needed for harmoniously posture, as national saying says: "Work as if you lived forever, but pray as if you died today" (584).

According to Biser (1995, 301), we are today facing the question about modern "humanistic illusion". Either a human can rise above his own problems in order to solve them, or it means creating human-angel. With other words: Either the humankind can redeem itself or we need a Redeemer/Saviour. This is probably one of the most important and basic questions of modern a-theistic and a-gnostic civilization.

It is very obvious that suicide and genocide are phenomena based on modern era; both are related to the question of reconciliation. Reconciliation means an invitation of the Old Testament (3 Mz, 23), which encourages humans for cooperation, reconciliation and for the creation of sincere, solidary and basic circumstances for human beings and humankind. Without reconciliation, which would reconnect people we are more and more apart from each other, which results in loneliness, and as a result of this there is depression and then suicide. “To celebrate a life simply means to live it with others.” (Rifkin 2009, 165) Cooperation is a source of power and strengthens lives of everybody, and it is not an exclusion; that is why genocide is the consequence of exclusion of some nations, groups of people, which enrolled in completely competitive relations of modern society. Snyder (2012, 379-421) describes reasons that lead people to killing or mass murdering of nations and certain groups in the first half of 20th Century, a bloody century of Nazi and Soviet tyranny. The fight for supremacy, authority and enforcement, and unacceptable social mechanisms, obedience, fear, big and small revenge, envy and opportunism, and other deviations from normal humanity contributed to atrocities and genocides during this period.. Everywhere, the managers of human destinies created conditions necessary for carrying out their “major goals”, regardless the price of victims. Grossman (1995) describes in detail the dilemmas, their horrors and dispassion in promoting the objectives of the system’s goals, in which man was an object. Lambert Ehrlich described this mechanism in detail in his works *The Russian Bolshevism* (1936a) and *Bolshevism in China* (1936b). Everything and everybody were involved in a complex system of procedures by planners of the “anthropological changes” toward class or racial society of the so called “new” man.

Part III

Modern Myths

William Cavanaugh (2010) speaks of modern myths which announced the salvation of problems of humankind in the modern age. Many of them were or unfortunately still are a cause of mentioned suicidal and genocidal threats. The modern society is trying to solve these problems by establishing of new political, social and cultural measurements which are in some sense a replacement for the earlier (mediaeval) structures of society. The problem is that most of them are one-sided and burdened by lack of spiritual or virtue’s qualification of individuals for this task. The development of modernity was reached structurally, but lacks inner consistence, which could be good interpersonal relations, trust of citizens in the system, and readiness for the responsible acting in the public sphere. The last one is not possible without good spiritual or ethical condition of citizens. A decisive, responsible acting is needed by public figures, which seems to be lacking in these modern systems. In such a case we would not face financial and structural crisis as we face it now. These problems are very complex and many questions arise in relation to them. First of all we have to analyse these myths of modernity and then see which visions are still possible. “Modernity is unaccustomed to regarding political theory as mythological in character” (Cavanaugh 2010, 9). The ground lies in the dilemma mentioned by Rousseau:

"Man was born free, but it is everywhere in bondage" (Rousseau 1954, 2; Cavanaugh 2010, 9). To avoid these problems the modern liberal state is trying to develop a state theory in which individuals give their freedom to be preserved and coordinated by the state authority to prevent violent tensions among them. Cavanaugh stresses that the wars and other sideways of modernity were caused by these struggles for a modern liberal state (15-20), and the accusations for infectivity of this modern state were foisted to the religious violence (20-30). The modern liberal state has remained as an untouched myth that such a state would be the saviour of societal troubles. "Far from coming on the scene as peace-keeper, we have seen that the rise of the state was at the very root of the so-called 'religious' wars, directing with bloodied hands a new secular theatre of absolute power." (46) The state was no saviour but the cause of imperialistic struggles, which culminated in the totalitarian systems of 20th century.

The "myth of civil society as a free space" is a more complicated one. According to Cavanaugh (2010) it is supported by many religious societal thinkers like Michel Novak (53) and Jon Courtenay Murray (54-62) in a sense that the civil space will fill the empty space with virtues and spiritual dimension, but without inclusion of theological language in the public discourse. Cavanaugh rightly asserts that theological language could not be excluded if we want that theology functions in the society. Against the liberal doctrine he asserts too with the most of communitarians that the virtues should be named and implemented in practical political life if we want that they function in the public sphere (88).

The last one is the myth of globalization as Christianity. Cavanaugh sees it as a "spatial story" (116). In the sense of political theology it is going "towards Eucharistic counter-politics" (46). We cannot go in the details here, but we can summarize that Cavanaugh gives grounds for an open, public theological discussion and for questioning of the spiritual grounds and the open theological language. Can theology bring us new hope?

Toward new hope?

Skrimshire (2008, 1) notes: "At the end of his 2004 Peace Lecture in Manchester, Noam Chomsky was asked this question from the floor: 'Do you live in hope, or despair?' And his response was perhaps the most controversial thing he had said that afternoon: 'It doesn't matter, I mean whether you have hope or despair is kind of like a personal matter between you and your wife and children or something, maybe not even that, it just doesn't matter, you do exactly the same thing, whether you're optimistic or pessimistic, really doesn't matter, it's a subjective question'." Skrimshire comments Chomsky's observations in the sense that "to ignore hope on the theoretical level … is surely to jeopardize a potentially powerful understanding of its practice." We need to deal with hope to react to our complex individual and societal problems.

To do this, we must implement the theological/spiritual view of reality which will influence the daily life and be designated as a "Theo-politics". In the sense of biblical *kairos* there is needed a "fundamental *temporal* reorientation" (196). This includes the imperative for dialogue of politics with theology. Skrimshire is referring to Cavanaugh's (2010, 86) book *Theopolitical Imagination* in which he insists that the Church has to be open for the public sphere in the sense of opening new spaces of politics, economics, social practices etc. This makes possible a new societal practice, "is a sense of urgency in integrating religious concepts and categories for reconceiving political practices of hope" (Skrimshire 2008, 198). He is hoping of "re-enchantment of the world" and suggests that "we must explore the question of hope through a variety of political, philosophical and theological languages" (199). In this sense it is necessary to transcend the empirical boundaries and to open spiritual grounds of man. According to Cavanaugh this couldn't be a universalistic, but an interpersonal project. This is "a spatial story" as he understands the Christian Eucharist. We need concrete projects of working or resisting the established status, or to be able for a "physical resistance". In the words of Cavanaugh this is story which "seeks to unify rather than divide" (116): "I will argue that the *Catholica* enacted by Eucharist is not a place as such, but a story which performs certain spatial operations on places … Stories organize and link spaces in a narrative sequence. They not only move from one space to another, but more accurately construct spaces through the practices of characters who trace an itinerary through story." (116) This is not a global (universal) abstract space but concrete every-day space. To give hope means to deal with concrete human spaces to make possible to exchange the stories and to unify.

Or in the words of Skrimshire (201): "For Foucault's chosen context, the Soviet Gulag read the terrorizing and parabolizing effects of fear within the war of terror: We must open the eyes … to what enables people there, on the spot, to resist the Gulag, what makes it intolerable for them […].What is it that sustains them, what makes them stand and fight? […] The leverage against the Gulag is not in our heads, but in their bodies, their energy, what they say, think, and do."

There are always concrete people working towards unjust conditions in the society. The concrete Eucharist, the living faith and the practical oppression is a way against the subjugating of wo/men. The imagination of future, the openness for it means to deal with concrete reactions of society to prevent the total closeness of all possibilities which is the basis of genocide and suicide. With Skrimshire: "Albert Camus said that the only important question in philosophy was that of suicide, or, more precisely, whether or not life was worth living. My own investigations make it clear that the most important question facing society today is that of *political* suicide, which might also be described as the abandonment of imagination of future. A competing fantasy of the future operates today as a dominant security paradigm. A politics of fear. Today we inhabit, in a state of acquiescence, a terrorized present. How then, have these observations been the backdoor for investigating practices of hope? Camus' reasoning proceeded from a kind of curiosity for how it is that the human spirit rebels in the face of the palpable absurdity of the world." (191) Or with the words of Cavanaugh (2010, 121): "On February, 13th, Fr. Rutilio Grande of El Salvador gave a homily during Mass in the villa of Apopa: 'The Lord gave us … a material world for all without borders….'". A human world is a world of dialogue and exchange of humanity and also of all earthly goods. This is a concrete, and not a universal (anonymous) Eucharist.

References

Biser, Eugen.1995. *Der Mensch – das uneingelöste Versprechen. Entwurf einer Modalanthropologie.* Düsseldorf: Pathmos.

Böckenförde, E. Wolfgang. 1976. *Staat, Gesellschaft, Freiheit. Studien zur Staatstheorie und zum Verfassungsrecht.* Frankfurt am Main: Suhrkamp.

Casanova, José. 2010. Säkularismus - Ideologie oder Staatskunst? In: *Transit. Europäische Revue.* Vienna: Verlag Neue Kritik, Nr. 39, 29–44.

Cavanaugh, William T. 2009. *The Myth of Religious Violence. Secular Ideology and the Roots of Modern Conflict.* Oxford: UP.

Cavanaugh, William T. 2010. *Theopolitical Investigation.* New York: T&T Clark.

Chomsky, Noam. 2004. Lecture at University of Manchester. Department of Government May 22th 2004. Sounded Out Films (DVD) (by Skrimshire 2008, 1).

Convention on the Prevention and Punishment of the Crime of Genocide (Convention)

Durkheim, Emil.1992. *Samomor. Prepoved incesta in njeni izzivi. (Suicide. Prohibition of Incest and its Challenges)* Ljubljana: Filoz. knjižnica Škuc, Studia humanitatis.

Ehrlich, Lambert.1936a. Ruski boljševizem (Russian Bolshevism). In: *ČAS* XVIII (1923/24), 192–217, 275–295.

Ehrlich, Lambert. 1936b. Boljševizem v Kini (Bolshevism in China). In: *Misijonski koledar* XVIII (1936), 97–99.

Foucault, Michel. 1980. *Powers and Strategies.* In: Colin Gordon(ed.), (trans. Colin Gordon and otheres), London: Harvester Press.

Genocide http://web.archive.org/web/20080502140534/http://www.unhchr.ch/html/menu3/b/p_genoci.htm; accessed on 1.8. 2013

Havel, Vaclav. 2012. Hoffnung . In: Limbeck, Meinrad. *Abschied vom Opfertod. Das Christentum neu entdecken.* Ostfildern: Mathias Grünewald (Schwaben), 11.

Judt, Tony/with Timothy Snyder. 2012. *Thinking Twentieth Century.* New York: Pinguin.

Milčinski, Lev. 1986. *Samomor in Slovenci (Suicide and Slovenes).* Ljubljana: CZ.

Pahor Boris. 2008. *Nekropola.* Ljubljana: MK

Rifkin Jeremy. 2009.*The Emhpatic Civilization. The Race to Global consciousness in a Worldin Crisis.* New York: Penguin.

Rousseau, Jean, Jacques. 1954. *The Socieal Contract* (trans. by Willmoore Kendall). South Bend, IN: Gateway Editions.

Skrimshire, Stefan. 2008. *Politics of Fear, Practice of Hope.* London: Continuum

Slovar slovenskega knjižnega jezika (*Vocabulary of Slovenian Literary Language, SSKJ*) I. 2000. Ljubljana: SAZU Inštitut Frana Ramovša.

Snyder, Thimothy. 2012. *Bloodlands. Europe between Hitler and Stalin*. New York: Basic Books.

Suicide. http://en.wikipedia.org/wiki/Suicide. Accessed 29.11. 2012

Šestov, Lev. 2002. *Dostojevski in Nietzsche*. Ljubljana: Literarno umetniško društvo: Literatura (zbirka Labirinti).

Trstenjak, Anton.1988. *Človek končno in neskončno bitje. Oznanjevalna antropologija (The Man, Final and Infinite Being. Anounce's Anthropology)*. Celje:MD

Wallach, Harald. 2011. *Spiritualität. Warum wir die Aufklärung weiterführen müssen*. Klein Yasedow: Drachen Verlag.

Welte, Bernhard.1982 Über die verschiedenen Bedeutungen des Nichts. In: Welte, Bernhard (ed.) *Zwischen Zeit und Ewigkeit. Abhandlungen und Versuche*. Freiburg (Br.), 43–50.

FACTORS AND INDICATORS OF GENOCIDE

Bojan Žalec, *Ljubljana*

1. Introduction

We can deal with genocide and its conditions and factors at different levels. In this essay I don't deal with it at the most basic level. At this level we can describe, approach and investigate genocide in terms of (violation of) solidary personalism (Žalec 2013), "elimination" of transcendence, assertion of certainty and anti-Christianity (Voegelin 1987), in terms of Kierkegaardian (Žalec 2014), Girardian terms and the similar. This fundamental level is level of philosophy and theology. But the present essay offers a synthetic survey of factors and indicators of genocide as they are revealed by many different scientific disciplines and a combination of them (by multidisciplinary approach): cultural anthropology, history, (social) psychology, science of politics etc. Its aim is to contribute - or make it easier - to integral picture and understanding of genocide (provided by this book).

2. "Introductory" list of indicators

We can start our survey by mentioning the following indicators (cf. Heindrich 2001: 73-85; Jones 2011, Ch. 16):

1) *Media which refill fuel to the fire* (wars start with words and pictures).

2) *Accumulation of weapons.*

3) *Increasing of violence, repression.* Here belongs: extended abuse or violation of human rights, increasing of a violent political repression, fast increasing of organized killing. The last indicator, before organized genocide starts, can be the start of a war or a rebellion or very intensive propaganda which present certain group (group identity) as a demonic enemy and push it into the position of a (public) scapegoat.

4) *(Growing) division, polarization.* The risk for genocide is bigger if a society is stratified in (potentially) opposite rival group identities.

5) *Cultivation of denying or hosting morality.* A further risk is a circumstance if at least one of groups cultivates morality of denying dignity of those who it considers its enemies, if cultivates e.g. mass contempt and hate. Such morality usually reflects quasi religious morality, as in the case of Nazism or communism.

6) *(Low) level of political culture.*[1]

[1] For the criteria and measuring of political culture cf. Kolenc 2002.

7) *Absolute power.* The society which is prone to genocide has little if any resources to limit or to cope with regime forces, or with other words, in dictator regimes there are more possibilities for genocide as in constitutional democracies. Therefore factors for dictatorship are also factors for genocide. Based on the book of Daniel Chirot *Modern Tyrants* (cf. especially pp. 409-420)[2] we can give the following statements about tyranny:

> a) Bigger the chaos on economical, legal and political field is and more it seems that relevant systems are not successful on these fields more probable is that there will appear a tyrant as a (self-proclaimed) savior.
>
> b) The more the management apparatus of a state is weak, the more probable it seems that there will spread a kind of chaos which leads to the appearance of a kind of a strong national savior and more easy will be for him to become a tyrant after he gets power.
>
> c) For each nation, new or old, we can assess a measure in which identity of its political and intellectual elite basis on jealousy and a revengeful resentment, on revengeful memory of previous mistakes, real and imagined, and we can assess more it is so greater is possibility of future tyrannies.
>
> d) The more the collective values take precedence over the rights of individuals and the more it is believed that every person is determined with characteristics which she automatically inherits from her community, the more probable it is that tyranny will seem more acceptable (because it is better for community).
>
> e) The stronger the ideologies of inevitable (unavoidable) conflict between communities are - there may be in question races, nations, economical classes or religions -, the more probable is that a tyranny will appear.
>
> f) Nationalism which is based on fear and resentment towards outer world which requires common solidarity of all nation regardless cultural or individual differences, and which is confronted with a serious inner ethnical and religious diversity, will probably be enforced by force. This will lead to a rebellion and consequently to the acceptance of increasing tyrannical methods of ruling of those who have the power in order to maintain nationalistic ideal.
>
> g) National elites which are sure that discipline and social purity, defined as exclusion of "foreign" values and habits, can save complex problems of adopting to modern world will probably become more and more frustrated and tyrannical when or if they come to the power.

---

[2] Although I must say that all Chirot`s statements do not seem entirely acceptable to me.

h) A tyrant who is not an intellectual or who ceases to be an intellectual and who refuses the influence of intelligence or intellectuals, he will spoil because his power will lack an adequate cultural and ethical foundation. He will feel threatened from intellectuals and he will prosecute them since they will have more coherent ideological programs which will endanger his power.

8) *History.* If in recent years there have been committed genocidal actions in certain society and the perpetrators were punished slightly or even have not been punished at all[3], there is a danger that such actions will be repeated. Actually those actions could be even terribly exceeded if in the past years the government has strengthened its power by violating – in a greater extent – human rights.

9) *Low or inadequate international support to the risk groups.* From the examples from the past we can infer an important political lesson: low or inadequate international support for target groups increases violence against them.

10) *Accepting or implementation of torturing.* It is very important that in societies prevails recognition that torturing people, even in the case of terrible criminals or in the case of very important information, is not acceptable. Torturing represents the most brutal and palpable instrumentalization of people and this is the basic evil and the basic element of any genocide. We must not succumb to Machiavellian temptations and craps if I use the words of Jacques Maritain (cf. Maritain 2002: 80), and we must not give priority to calculation or to use of a certain power instead to justice. Accepting of torture is "the best" way to enter the wheels of evil and at the same time a sign that we have already slid into it. The importance of refusing and condemning of torture cannot be overestimated. This becomes even clearer if we are aware of the correctness of the dissonance theory (I will briefly explain it further on).

3. Education, personal growth, (self)reflection and care[4]

Besides the above factors we should stress the importance of education, development in width and depth and (self)reflection. So we must for example be aware that it is difficult for us to attribute genocidal acts to those groups which enjoy our sympathies and that strong "self-censorship" is necessary. Traveling and learning about others are also very important. We must strive for checking of authorities and for preventing of genocidal powers which are on the way, for getting the relevant information regarding genocides and their consequences

[3] For the importance of punishment regarding the prevention of evil see Kekes 2005, especially pages 240-242. Punishment of perpetuators is also a condition for reconciliation: "Further, reconciliation can take place after the wrongdoer has suffered punishment, in contrast to the exercise of mercy." (Harak 2007, 1134)

[4] Cf. Jones 2011: 599-601.

(also, but not only in our country), and for taking sanctions against genocidal actions and their agents or perpetrators.[5]

4. Sources of information about genocide[6]

a) Besides *satellites* it is worth to mention *open source reporting* and *open-source intelligence* (OSINT) information. This source (media, internet etc.) demands trained expert otherwise the person who is searching will be swamped with irrelevant information and she will have difficulties to distinguish between relevant and not-relevant information.

b) Hostile literature and propaganda. First publicly available indicator of genocidal intentions of a certain group may be its ideological literature. The literature of Nazis, Marxists and Leninists, Arabic Baathists, Ruanda "Hutu Power" or Serbian extreme nationalists has emerged years before they committed genocides, and years before they gained political power. If we read for example Hitler`s *Mein Kampf* we can realize that it expresses hate, tyrannical conception and anti-Semitism. But it may also happen that one group does not express its genocidal tendencies before it comes to power. But when they come to power even the most silent groups must express their genocidal propaganda to propagate their aims. This propaganda may be mixed with talking about peace or directed only to the right public: so in Ruanda anti-Tutsi directed radio broadcasted only in the language of locals, whereas more conciliatory speaking which misled foreign listeners was broadcasted in French. Nevertheless the core of hostile propaganda exists, it is publicly available and it may be a very important factor when we try to discern a danger of genocide. It may also directly declare genocidal intentions of groups or regimes and it may reveal the target groups of genocidal intentions.

c) *News in media.* Most of modern genocides were discovered or revealed thanks to news in international media. At one side we may expect that genocidal regimes will not allow freedom of the press. But on the other side even totalitarian and very autocratic states have tolerated the presence of foreign correspondents, including Nazi Germany, the Soviet Union, Iran under Khomeini and even Hussein`s Iraq. Besides, in the countries where there is at least some freedom of media the best correspondents are local journalists. They know how to act in their country, they follow its social and political trends, and they are often prepared to research sensitive political stories regardless danger. For timely discovering of genocides TV is not the right media. When news is ready to be used on TV, genocide is already a (blossoming) fact. A bigger range and depth and

---

[5] Not-sanctioned crimes are an important (outer) factor which helps to increase evil. About inner factors or reasons (which include unreal, false presentations which makes people able to commit crimes, including genocide) and outer factors of evil cf. Kekes 2005 (especially chapters 12-15), and Žalec 2005, 40 ff.

[6] Cf. Heidenrich 2001: 74-79.

temporally more appropriate usefulness have newspapers even though they are also under market and political pressures. Besides journalist usually publish only a part of what they know or what they suspect, even if there is no censorship.

d) *NGOs and religious groups or communities.* Religious groups are the first to know about persecution on religious basis especially if their members are in question. So the Roman Catholic Church is a network which is global, present almost in every country.

e) *International organizations.* These organizations, most apparently within the UN, give further possible sources for early warnings about genocide. The UN has its employees all over the world. The UN has its special reporters. For some countries with very disreputable regimes there are special reporters for special fields: for human rights, for genocide problems, for religious intolerance, for modern forms of racism, xenophobia and similar intolerance, for non-legal and other fast executions, for torturing, for violence against women, for sale of children, for child prostitution and child pornography, for independence of the judiciary. Most of the reports are publicly available. Many agreements about human rights demand yearly reports about fighting against "evils" from the states parties to the agreements.

f) *Academy.* By this are meant independent research organizations and also universities. With this are not important only political scientists, but also philosophers, sociologists, professors of law, criminologists, anthropologists and also theologians. Their findings are worth to be taken into account.

5. Anthropology, psychology and essentialization[7]

"Most of you know what it means to see a hundred corpses lying together, five hundred or a thousand. To have gone through this and yet – apart from a few exceptions, examples of human weakness – remained decent, this has made us hard."

Heinrich Himmler in his speech given to the leaders of SS who were in charge to kill Jews, 1943[8]

Are we murderers or peaceful people? We must beware of every too simplified view on man and his nature. Man as such is neither beast nor angel, but ambivalent being who bears potentials for good and bad (evil). Furthermore, man is a being of adaption and of imitation, and that is why the environment and conditions are so important for his acting. Evidence about genocides proves that perpetrators of genocides are not beasts, but many of them are ordinary people who have became (mass) murderers due to special conditions. Therefore we must mostly and in the first place condemn system and conditions and we must take

[7] Cf. Chirot & McCauley 2006, Ch. 2.

[8] Chirot & McCauley 2006, loc. 986-94.

into consideration both also by judging and punishing of perpetrators. Chirot & McCauley (2006, loc. 429-432 ff; 989-95) expose four main motives or reasons for genocides: greed for material benefits and political ambitions (their term for this first group is *convenience* (loc. 441-45 ff)), revenge (loc. 519-22 ff; 538-42 ff), simple fear (loc. 643-64 ff), and fear of "contamination" or "pollution" (loc. 724-727 ff). These reasons are often intertwined. For instance, many of those who supported genocide against the Cherokee Indians did not want only material benefits but they were also racists. The most fatal is maybe the fourth reason since it is based on the attitude that only the presence of the focused group is so dangerous that it is necessary to eliminate it. On a dinner with Himmler (22nd February 1942) Hitler said that discovery of Jewish virus was one of the greatest revolutions in the world and the fight that "we" fought was really the same as that of Pasteur and Koch (cf. Chirot & McCauley 2006, loc. 378-83).

Our understanding of genocides is still very incomplete (imperfect) and our explanation must be (psychologically) supplemented. An essential part of this demands understanding of how an ordinary man can become a mass murderer (cf. op. cit., 1008-12 ff).[9]

Very important are leaders and emotions. There are very rare genocides without a central leadership. The analysis about expenses and benefits can explain a lot regarding the views and acting of leaders, but at the same time it leaves many questions opened. Leaders are, like those who they lead, subjected to emotions and this may lead them much further and away from utilitarian rationality.

Mass killings of large dimensions are a consequence of passions and ideologies which have lasted for longer (cf. op. cit., 1149-52 ff). It is very dangerous if political dreams prevail over (economic) reality which happened in the cases of communism and Nazism. Jon Elster (1999: 306) wrote that short-lasting passions undermine the theory about man as a rational actor, and long-lasting passions the one about *homo economicus*. Which are the most relevant passions and emotions which have brought so much sorrow and pain?

Certainly fear (cf. Chirot & McCauley 2006, loc. 1161-65 ff)[10] is the key emotion for understanding of genocide. Then we must mention anger or wrath (op. cit., loc. 1250-54 ff).[11] Then hate (op. cit., loc. 1356-59 ff). Among theories about hate the theory of the psychologist Robert Sternberg (2003) has a big explanatory power. He suggested a threefold theory of hate which includes: contempt, disgust, and a mixture of anger (wrath) and fear. The opposite to hate is love (op. cit. 1407-10 ff). Anger (wrath) is of more passive, reactive nature and is shorter, whereas hate is more active and stabile emotion which may be also

---

[9] Regarding this question cf. also Dežman 2008.

[10] For a complex and multidisciplinary consideration of the culture of fear see Juhant & Žalec (eds.) 2013.

[11] For deeper understanding of the role of thymos, wrath, anger and similar emotions and passions in (political) history cf. Sloterdijk 2008.

cold. A positive or a negative identification with a group is also of an essential importance since group identification is a psychological base of an intergroup conflict. As a reason for genocide there are often mentioned shame and humiliation (cf. op. cit., loc. 1466-70 ff). Both, shame[12] and humiliation comprise public loss of respect, appreciation and status. But the difference depends on if it is considered as deserved or not deserved. In numerous genocides perpetrators try to lessen the humanity of victims and they proclaim them for animals, for infective and for very dirty. They cultivate the feeling of disgust (cf. op. cit. 1506-10 ff) towards them. These emotions and views are connected with the essentialization of the other (cf. op. cit. 1529-32 ff; 1532-35 ff).

The idea of essence which is shared by all members of the target group is of crucial importance for explaining genocidal violence against groups, especially if in question is a dangerous similarity of the other (e.g. Catholics and Protestants).

We must take into account also dissonance[13] theory (cf. Sabini 1995) which takes all people as inclined to adapt our convictions (believes) to our (already done) actions. This fact triggers a mechanism of interactive dialectics between convictions (believes) and actions: the commission of a certain crime triggers an adequate change of believes, these believes allow new (even worse) crimes which again trigger a change of believes etc. Therefore it is very important - if we want to stop a vicious circle of this dialectics – that a person admits to herself and to others that some of her actions were bad, wrong, since this is the only way of redemption from the wheels of evil, described by the dissonance theory.[14]

Besides the mentioned emotions and factors, organization (cf. Chirot & McCauley 2006, loc. 1095-99 ff), routine and habits or obedient psyche are very important. Alienation, too technicized world, too much bureaucracy, absence of a direct contact between murderers and victims also play certain role. These factors are for some also the basis for difference between genocides of the 20th cen-

---

[12] For the analysis of shame in the context of reconciliation – which is of course of enormous importance for overcoming of the consequences of genocides – see Strahovnik 2012.

[13] “Dissonance is an unpleasant arousal that comes from seeing ourselves as having chosen to do something wrong, stupid, or sleazy – that is, something at odds with our positive self-image”. (Chirot & McCauley 2006, loc. 1045-47)

[14] Accepting of the dissonance theory can be also a basis for the claim about harmfulness of inhuman penalties, e.g. death penalty, since the feeling of responsibility for executions can cause people to accept dangerous claims about the nature of some (punished) people: that they are not persons, that they are incurable and completely evil, that revenge is something good etc. Such convictions again increase danger of new crimes.

tury and those before (Hannah Arendt (1962; 1992), Zygmunt Bauman (1995)).[15]

It is important to mention that shock of direct contact with victims lasts only for short time, and afterwards an important percentage of people get used to killing and it becomes a routine to them. Even for the notorious leader of the SS Heinrich Himmler the first contact with the killing of Jews was a hard experience. The same we can infer from the book *Soldaten* (Neitzel & Welzer 2011). Similar it is true of pictures of atrocities in the mass media. But on the other hand we must - especially in today technologically very sophisticated world - cultivate intellectual control over our actions and we must be aware of the consequences of our actions though we do not perceive them directly. We must be aware what it means to drop a bomb on Hiroshima though we will not be present to see the destruction it will cause. In other words we need intellectual reflection, we need ethics. (Cf. McCabe 2005, 112-113)

Ways to genocide are different and only some of the requirements for it which have been mentioned are necessary. Essentialization of the other is essential but there are many ways how it goes on.[16] In addition the essentialisation of "enemy" may be necessary but it is not enough for genocide. (Chirot & McCauley 2006, loc. 1688-91) From social-psychological experiments and from actual experience of mass killings we know that we can make ordinary people to commit atrocities even if they have not negative emotions towards victims. Recalling of stereotypes, fear, anger and hate can even make killing easier and accelerate it. We have already stressed the importance of organization in the understanding of genocide: habits of obeying, structure of everyday organizational incentives, specialization, routine which undermines personal responsibility or feeling for it. These aspects of organization can promote mass killings also in the absence of strong negative emotions or feelings to victims. Fear from consequences if you do not kill, including fear from death, is another example of how to motivate perpetrators of crimes. (Cf. op. cit., 1693-1701)

Leaders, heads who direct genocidal conditions are something else than ordinary perpetrators. They are those who make complicated justifications or "ra-

---

[15] This opinion of Arendt and Bauman is shared by Janez Juhant who wrote: "In the past hate could hardly get such dimensions as it is possible with the achievements of new technology. Sophisticated, in detail designed media strategic-propaganda planes even today mobilize masses against newly created class social enemies. As convincingly showed Hannah Arendt (2003) and Zygmunt Bauman (2006) the modern technological society allowed, in this context, strategies of mass destruction of opponents." (Juhant 2010: 16) For the criticism of the modernist view on genocide (Arendt, Bauman) see Chirot & McCauley, loc. 415-18 ff, especially loc. 423-26 ff. Modernism about genocides claims that there is something special or essentially different on modern genocides (cf. ibid.).

[16] "In short, it seems that almost any kind of social category will do, as long as it can be considered self-reproducing" (Chirot & McCauley 2006, loc. 1546-48).

tionalization" of that what is happening, especially if the victims of genocide are very similar to those who carry out killings. Let us remember complicated explanations why the Vietnamese in Kampuchea, Trotskyites, Tutsis must be killed, why Protestants/Catholics are dangerous heretics even though their religion is so similar to the Catholic/Protestant one. These explanations must have been given and justified by intellectuals who look into the issues. On the level of elites we can most clearly see human inclination to historize our fears and rage, our hate and love, and to cultivate our resentments - because of our previous humiliation or mistakes - and to (or we may even (sometimes) say in order to) redirect them to revenge actions. (Op. cit. 1701-1714) Comparison of the leaders and the perpetrators reveals that negative emotions to enemies are often much stronger in the leaders than in those who actually perform genocide. In the speech of elites we find the strongest evidence for wrath, fear, hate, humiliation and disgust directed towards enemies. We must be aware that it is not just rhetoric and that "successful" leaders often believe to their own words, they believe in the emotions expressed by those words. We may say that hate is more appropriate explanation when talking about elites than when talking about ordinary people or followers. (Op. cit. 1714-1721)

On the other side it is much more complex task to understand the psychology of ordinary perpetrators (not leaders) since there is less material and they are not prepared to talk. It is more difficult to understand their calculations, ideologies, fears, hate and resentments than those of their leaders. This is especially difficult when crimes were committed without any organized central authority and in the case of neighbors, villagers etc. In these cases we cannot blame orders, the fact that we were soldiers and that this was an act of solidarity in a strange environment etc. (Cf. op. cit. 1721-33) In such cases the crimes were committed in a way voluntary. Such example is described in the book of Jan Gross *Neighbors*. In a half-Catholic and half-Jewish town Jedwabne, Polish "Catholics" killed approximately 1600 Jewish men, women and children soon after the German occupation in 1941 (before the town was occupied by Soviets). Similar happened in some other Polish towns. Chirot and McCauley conclude: "In fact, without substantial Polish collaboration, the Nazis would not have been able to slaughter about 90 percent of Poland's three million Jews." (Op. cit., 1736-39)

6. Conclusion

Factors of genocide are only one part (already itself very complex) of a complete and complex picture of genocide. Yet they are in one sense its most central part because without knowledge about them no other part of the picture of genocide (its conceptual analysis and definition, its discerning from the similar phenomena (mass murders, crime against humanity etc.)[17], strategies to prevent it or to decrease the chances of it, coping with its consequences etc.) can be

[17] About these topics see Žalec 2013.

provided in a grounded, verified and efficient way. Of course the list of these factors cannot be used as a kind of simple way for recognition and understanding of genocides. This list is just a mean which should help us by our very careful and "particularistic" consideration of every particular situation or case. With this warning against searching for "certain" and too easy ways to recognize and understand genocides I conclude this survey. False certainty and lack of modesty are not only positive factors of genocides, but also obstacles to understand and prevent them and to cure their effects.

References

Arendt, Hannah. 1962. *The Origins of Totalitarianism*. London: G. Allen & Unwin.

Arendt, Hannah. 1992. *Eichmann in Jerusalem: a report on the banality of evil*. New York etc.: Penguin Books.

Arendt, Hannah. 2003. *Izvori totalitarizma* (trans. Zdenka Erbežnik, Patricija Fajon, Polona Glavan). Ljubljana: Študentska založba.

Arendt, Hannah. 2007. *Eichmann v Jeruzalemu* (trans. Polona Glavan). Ljubljana: Študentska založba.

Bauman, Zygmunt. 1995. *Modernity and the Holocaust*. Cambridge: Polity Press.

Bauman, Zygmunt. 2006. *Moderna in holokavst* (trans. Slavica Jesenovec Petrović in Borut Petrović Jesenovec). Ljubljana: Študentska založba.

Chirot, Daniel. 1994. *Modern Tyrants: The Power and Prevalence of Evil in Our Age*. Princeton, New Jersey: Princeton University Press.

Chirot, Daniel & McCauley, Clark. 2006. *Why Not Kill Them All? The Logic and Prevention of Mass Political Murder*. Princeton and Oxford: Princeton University Press.

Dežman, Jože. 2008. Tranzicijska pravičnost (Transitional justice). In: Jože Dežman (ed.) *Poročilo Komisije Vlade Republike Slovenije za reševanje vprašanj prikritih grobišč 2005–2008*. Ljubljana: Družina, pp. 251–428.

Elster, Jon. 1999. *Alchemies of the Mind: Rationality and Emotions*. Cambridge: Cambridge University Press.

Gross, Jan Tomasz. 2001. *Neighbors: The Destruction of the Jewish Community in Jedwabne, Poland*. Princeton, NJ: Princeton University Press.

Harak, Simon G. S. J. 2007. Reconciliation. In: Orlando O. Espín & James B. Nickoloff (eds.), *An Introductory Dictionary of Theology and Religious Studies*. Dublin: The Columbia Press.

Hitler, Adolf. 2006. *Moj boj = Mein Kampf:* dve knjigi združeni v eni knjigi (trans. Marjan Furlan). Celje: Mavrica.

Heidenrich, John G. 2001. *How to Prevent Genocide: A Guide for Policymakers, Scholars, and the Concerned Citizen*. Westport, Connecticut in London: Praeger.

Jones, Adam. 2011[2] (2006[1]). *Genocide: A Comprehensive Introduction*. London & New York: Routledge.

Juhant, Janez. 2010. Človek – ovira samemu sebi na poti dialoga (Man – an obstacle to him/herself on the way of dialogue). In: Janez Juhant & Bojan Žalec (eds.), *Na poti k dialoški človeškosti*. Ljubljana: Teološka fakulteta, pp. 11–23.

Juhant, Janez & Žalec, Bojan (eds.). 2013. *From Culture of Fear to Society of Trust*. Zürich & Berlin: Lit 2013.

Kekes, John. 2005. *The Roots of Evil*. Ithaca & London: Cornell University Press.

Kolenc, Janez. 2002. *Politična kultura na prehodu v demokracijo (primer Slovenije)* <Political culture in the transition into democracy (the case of Slovenia)>. Ljubljana: i2.

Maritain, Jacques. 2002. *Človek in država* (orig. *Man and the State*, trans. Cirila Toplak). Ljubljana: Študentska založba.

McCabe, Herbert. 2005. *The Good Life: Ethics and the Pursuit of Happiness.* London & New York: Continuum.

Neitzel, Sönke & Welzer, Harald. 2011. *Soldaten. Protokolle vom Kämpfen, Töten und Sterben*. Frankfurt: S. Fischer.

Sabini, John. 1995. *Social Psychology*. New York: W. W. Norton.

Sloterdijk, Peter. 2008. *Zorn und Zeit. Politisch-psychologischer Versuch*. Frankfurt: Suhrkamp Verleg.

Sternberg, Robert J. 2003. A Duplex Theory of Hate: Development and Applications to Terrorism, Massacres, and Genocide. *Review of General Psychology* 7 (3), pp. 299–328.

Strahovnik, Vojko. 2012. Guilt, Shame and Reconciliation within the Context of Humanity. In: Janez Juhant & Bojan Žalec (eds.). *Reconciliation: The Way of Healing and Growth*. Zürich & Münster: Lit, pp. 129-137.

Voegelin, Eric. 1987. *The New Science of Politics: An Introduction.* Chicago & London: The University of Chicago Press.

Žalec, Bojan. 2005. *Doseganje dobrega* (Reaching of Good). Ljubljana: Študentska založba.

Žalec, Bojan. 2013. Genocide as Social Death: A Comparative Conceptual Analysis. *Anthropological Notebooks*, year 19, no. 2, pp. 57-74.

Žalec, Bojan. 2014. Nazism and Stalinism in the Light of Kierkegaard's Thought. *Filozofia*, year 69, no. 5, pp. 443-450.

DESPAIR AND SUICIDE. A KIERKEGAARDIAN REFLECTION

Branko Klun, *Ljubljana*

One of the fundamental existential topics in Kierkegaard's thought is the notion of despair. We may be inclined to think that intensified despair eventually leads to the problem of suicide, but this is not the case with Kierkegaard. He only gives the topic of suicide brief consideration, and he does not link the problem of despair primarily with that of ending one's own life. Nevertheless, Kierkegaard's analysis of human existence can provide us with important clues to more successfully deal with the phenomenon of suicide, which is often the consequence of an intensive state of despair. The term *suicide* comes from the Latin *sui-cidium*, the killing of oneself, which is also translated as *self-slaughter* (Kierkegaard 1941, 72-73). Our usual understanding of this word is centred on the notion of killing or slaughtering, whereas the word *self* merely represents a reflexive pronoun without a deeper meaning. However, an existential analysis of Kierkegaard demands that we change this perspective and focus on the word *self*. The problem of *self-killing* must first search for an appropriate understanding of the *self*, which can by no means be reduced to the empirical fact of one's physical identity. In the light of a new understanding of the *self*, the question of physically ending life receives a secondary role. *Thus, the aim of this paper is to present the importance of this methodological shift, which displaces our attention from the final event of committing suicide to the question of the living and despairing self, which can be "lost" prior to its physical death.* The reversal of the traditional approach to suicide in the Kierkegaardian perspective can only be understood against the background of his methodological and anthropological presuppositions, which I will present in this article with the aid of the first few pages of *Sickness unto Death* (1941, 17-19) where, according to Tilo Wesche, we find the "nucleus of Kierkegaard's anthropology" (2003, 87).

The methodological presuppositions of Kierkegaard's thought

Like in any great philosophical thought, the originality of Kierkegaard lies in the fact that he opens up a new perspective and makes a new methodological approach possible. For Kierkegaard the absolute starting point for any questioning or understanding is our lived life, our concrete existence, which we experience *from within* and which can never be adequately understood *from without*. He refuses the possibility of an external perspective, something which is treated as a given by empirical science, which tries to objectify every phenomenon and transform it into the object of an uninvolved observer. Lived existence in a first-person perspective is the primary and insurmountable horizon from which any knowledge originates, and to which that same knowledge ultimately returns. This existence is not a static condition, but a dynamic activity. Every kind of understanding or knowledge – even knowledge of a particular object – is an activity performed by life, and the activity itself subsequently influences that very life. The purpose of knowing and understanding is embedded in the performance of life (Ricoeur 1998, 22), and while this life has no other purpose than to accomplish itself, the ultimate realisation of life can be interpreted in various ways. This methodological approach is diametrically opposed to the scientific method, which attempts to overcome the conditions of subjective life in order to gain objective knowledge.

What are the consequences of an existential methodology with regard to the question of suicide? It is quite evident that this question cannot be dealt with by means of the scientific approach, which defines suicide (from the outside) as an objective incident – when a person kills himself – but rather it must be dealt with from the perspective of lived life, in which someone relates to the possibility of self-killing. The first-person perspective does not mean falling into subjective arbitrariness, and it looks for general and invariant determinations of the analysed phenomenon. An example of such a phenomenological approach is given in Heidegger's analysis of death in *Being and Time*. From the perspective of a life which I live from within, the phenomenon of death appears as a pure possibility which will never become an actuality *for me* (as soon as my death becomes *actual* I no longer exist). Thus, death reveals itself as my "ownmost" and the "uttermost" possibility (Heidegger 1986, 294). Possibility, however, should not be understood as inferior to actuality; for Heidegger the being (of a human or *Dasein*) *is* a (performed) possibility, and for this reason death determines the very "essence" of my being. Similar to Heidegger's existential analysis, which was largely inspired by Kierkegaard (Anz 1998, 49), we can characterise suicide as a possibility which affects everyone in the uniqueness of their own existence. We can also draw some preliminary conclusions. Prior to the actual (objective) event of suicide, an individual thinks about it; he considers the possibility of putting end to his life. Suicide "lives" in the life of such a person before it is "actualised"; suicide is performed by a living person. This simple observation requires a methodological shift in perspective: from the act (and actuality) of suicide to the prior lived understanding of (the possibility of) suicide, which represents a certain way (or mode) of life.

In this perspective the phenomenon of despair plays an important role. Despair, which should be treated equally next to other uttermost possibilities of life, can bring forward and stimulate a decision about suicide. However, we should not forget that suicide can also have other reasons and motivations. Stoic philosophy, for example, regards suicide as the highest act of freedom (Seneca 1999, 11). Nevertheless, Kierkegaard interprets even a freely chosen death as a form of despair, but in order to understand his views on despair we have to first explain his analysis of the self.

Kierkegaard's anthropology and the question of the self

The famous summary of Kierkegaard's anthropology in the first chapter of *Sickness unto Death* (1941) begins with following sentences: "Man is spirit. But what is spirit? Spirit is the self. But what is the self? The self is a relation which relates itself to its own self, or it is that in the relation [which accounts for it] that the relation relates itself to its own self; the self is not the relation but [consists in the fact] that the relation relates to its own self" (Kierkegaard 1941, 17). At his very core, man is not a given and opaque reality (in spite of being physically present in the world), but a "relation". This can be understood in the perspective from within, where I experience myself through a specific "self"-understanding, or "self"-feeling. The self is constituted in this self-relating; it is (it performs itself as) a lived relation. There is a fundamental difference between the external reality of my body which belongs to the order of *actuality* and my internal existence – which can be called the life of the spirit – where even my bodily reality is experienced from within, and where my own self is experienced as a lived *possibility* (of a relation which relates to its own self).

To characterise the self as a relation means to introduce freedom into the very core of personal existence. Who I am (myself) is not a given and immutable fact (like the name on my identity card), but rather a task for my freedom – I have to become myself. This also implies the possibility that I can live (and relate to myself) in such a way that I am *not* myself; that I lead an inauthentic life in which *I lose myself.* A pure physical reality does not have the possibility of not being itself. An animal cannot, strictly speaking, *not* be itself. Only man is a lived relation (relating to himself); something which, phenomenologically, can also be called an "openness" (to oneself), and it is for this reason that he can be defined as spirit. In man the "I" and the "self" do not coincide in a simple way. "I" can live in such a way that I do not attain my true "self". To lose one's own self does not mean to end one's existence or to die. Nevertheless, for Kierkegaard such a loss of one's own self is a greater difficulty than one's physical death.

To define man as a performed, lived relation to himself is, however, not the last truth about him. Kierkegaard writes: "Such a relation which relates itself to its own self (that is to say, a self) must either have constituted itself or have been constituted by another" (1941, 18). According to him, the human self is "a derived, constituted relation" by the Creator (Kierkegaard 1941, 18). For these reasons, relating to one's own self never remains a task which is closed within itself, but it simultaneously relates itself to another, i.e. to God. It would be wrong to interpret these two relations (to one's own self and to God) as separate, because in essence they are connected (Derrida 1995, 109). Not until I become my true self (i.e. truly myself) do I have an authentic relation to God and vice versa. To be in the "relation to the Power which constituted" myself (Kierkegaard 1941, 19) implies to have an external measure, or criterion, of what my true or genuine self is. Otherwise, how can I truly know that I have fully realised myself, and not just fallen into a vicious cycle of a self-deceit?

It is precisely through a relation to this transcendent Power which internally constitutes me that the task of *becoming I myself* receives a dimension of eternity and, thus, an infinite seriousness. My freedom is not a playful choice wherein I can arbitrarily design myself and change my mind at any time; it carries within itself a fundamental responsibility. I have to respond to the Power that preceded me, and I have to build or edify my true self with a continuous and never-ending effort. For Kierkegaard, the burden of this responsibility is the actual source of despair.

The phenomenon of despair and the question of death

The discrepancy – what Kierkegaard also calls "disrelationship" (1941,19) – between the task of attaining the true self and the ever-present danger of losing one's authentic self forms the basis of the phenomenon of despair. It is clear from the outset that the ultimate consequence of despair is not death, but the loss of the self; my failure of truly being myself. According to Kierkegaard, death is not an ultimate possibility of existence which cannot be outstripped, as in Heidegger's secularised version of Kierkegaard's existential analysis (Heidegger 1986, 264), and as such death does not have the final word about life. For this reason suicide, in the sense of giving death to oneself, does not play the kind of role in Kierkegaard's thinking that we might expect. The secret of despair is deeper than death, and it goes beyond it – unless we interpret death metaphorically, as in a "death of spirit" or the "loss of the self".

In *Sickness unto Death* Kierkegaard differentiates among various kinds of despair, and undertakes a meticulous analysis of each of them. First, he makes a distinction between what we could call authentic and inauthentic despair. Inauthentic despair is an unconscious despair which someone is not truly aware of. This ordinary notion of despair is considered to be a transitory state, which should be overcome. An example of this could be the despair of a girl who has been left by her fiancé. This despair is not concerned with truly becoming oneself and as a pure emotion it hinders the appearance of authentic despair. According to Kierkegaard authentic despair has two basic forms, depending on whether man acknowledges his relationship to the transcendent Power (God) or not. If there is no relationship to transcendence, despair remains closed within the immanence of self-relation (between *I* and *myself*) with no reference to some kind of external authority. For Kierkegaard the absence of such an authority explains the pagan attitude to suicide:

> "Hence it came about [...] that the pagans judged self-slaughter so lightly, yea, even praised it, notwithstanding that for the spirit it is the most decisive sin, that to break out of existence in this way is rebellion against God. [...] He lacked the point of view for regarding self-slaughter, he lacked the God-

> relationship and the self. From a purely pagan point of view self-slaughter is a thing indifferent, a thing every man may do if he likes, because it concerns nobody else." (1941, 72-73)

In this form of despair man refuses to be what he is, he "is not willing to be oneself" (Kierkegaard 1941, 78). Kierkegaard undertakes a thorough differentiation of the various levels and reasons for the refusal of the self, ranging from the pure weakness of not being able to accept the self, to despair as a defiance and insistence on one's own miserable existence. However, all these forms of despair do not attain the full notion of despair, which comes about from an awareness in which I find myself in a relationship with a transcendent Power. From the religious perspective, despair is experienced as a sin, where this sin is not a single action, but a permanent state of man (sinfulness) in the presence of God (*coram Deo*). Only after acknowledging the relation to God is the self revealed in all its greatness. God becomes the measure for the genuine self. For Kierkegaard, it is precisely the experience of not being able to attain my true self in its deepest dimension (in its eternal meaning, coming from the relation to God) that represents the basis for the highest form of despair. This despair cannot be overcome by increasing efforts in developing an ethically virtuous self, but solely by faith. Faith means trusting God to be the ultimate basis and the deepest affirmation of my own self. In faith, my centre is moved from myself to God, and it is precisely in this dis-possesion (of the self) that the true self is attained. The eradication of despair, which is also "the formula for believing", takes place when "by relating itself to its own self, and by willing to be itself, the self is grounded transparently in the Power which constituted it" (Kierkegaard 1941, 77-78). The relation to the self and the relation to God are not mutually exclusive but, rather, are complementary. Such a faith or believing represents the realisation of myself; it represents the eternity (the eternal self) which is lived and experienced within the temporality of life.

Despair is not a sickness which, like bodily sicknesses, could end in death. To be spirit, something which for Kierkegaard is equal to being the self, means to have a dimension of eternity. What I become (i.e. my self) has an eternal meaning. Despair, according to Kierkegaard, is a sickness of the "I", who despairs over the inability of becoming itself, and who even has a desire for self-annihilation. But, this can never happen, and this is precisely because the spirit or the self is eternal, and the impossibility of death (as annihilation) makes the despair even deeper. The sickness unto death in this case represents the painful paradox, "everlastingly to die and yet not to die", where the "last hope, death, is not available" (1941, 25). From the religious perspective death does not have the last word, and it is not the primary negation of life either. Much more dangerous is the other "loss" of life – the loss of the self; or not becoming my self. My death cannot erase my authentic self, yet the contrary is possible: even my death can become an event of my authentic self. However, this event can never be suicide. For Kierkegaard, self-killing is possible only if I am not in relationship with God. Otherwise, I am aware that suicide represents an upheaval against the Power which constituted me, and that even death does not absolve me from the eternal responsibility, which I have towards myself.

Beyond the religious paradigm

Can Kierkegaard's reflections have relevance in our present time, which is characterised by a reluctance to accept a transcendent Power as the basis of one's own self? An attempt to conduct an existential analysis, which seeks to understand human existence solely from itself, and with no relation to God, has already been undertaken by Heidegger. It is interesting that Heidegger does not deal with the issue of suicide, despite the fact that the phenomenon of death plays a crucial role in his existential analysis. Nevertheless, Heidegger was able to explore many of Kierkegaard's existential "categories" and to show their timeless relevance. Even today we can still build upon Kierkegaard's methodology and use his terminology for describing the complex phenomenon of suicide. However, in this conclusion I would only like to provide some basic outlines and ideas.

Every suicide is a refusal of one's own self, and this refusal is lived before the actual suicide takes place. The refusal of one's self reveals the despair over oneself, which basically means the inability of someone to be himself, or just to truly or genuinely "be". The loss of one's own self (an inauthentic existence) reflects a specific understanding, because self-understanding (as a lived relation to one's self) is inseparably bound to life. Every understanding and its corresponding way (or mode) of life represents one of the *possibilities* of the self, which is a different name for human freedom. When I live in an inauthentic way, when I lose myself, I know that there is another possibility (and that I am even obliged to choose such a possibility of my true self). It is possible to *be* differently; to exist in a genuine sense, and to truly become myself. Despair always emerges from a discrepancy between the actual state of my "fallen" life and a vocation to my genuine existence. In this context Heidegger emphasises the importance of the conscience, which calls me from this "fallenness" (1986, 270) to my authentic existence.

The main problem here concerns precisely the call of conscience, or the criterion of how to recognise a certain way of life as authentic, as an expression of my true self. How can I discern between my true and my false self? My understanding (of myself) may be heavily influenced by other people and their value judgments. In that case, the attainment of one's own self would be measured according to acceptance or refusal by others (and it is known that negative public judgment about someone is often one of the reasons for suicide). Heidegger stresses the importance of detaching oneself from public opinion (the "They") and listening to one's own voice of conscience. However, here Kierkegaard's question remains crucial: Am I alone the measure for myself, can I really find the answer about my true self within the immanence of my isolated existence? Or, is the ultimate measure for my authentic self my relation to the transcendent Power? Does my temporal existence have the last word about itself, or does it have a relation to an eternal and absolute reference, revealing a much deeper responsibility towards myself?

Speaking about eternity with regard to the self should not be interpreted as an eternal ideal (of the self), which is posited in advance as a final goal of my life or of myself. Rather, we should reverse the perspective: in my actual and concrete life I make decisions which have an eternal meaning. In the effort of becoming myself, in every decision, I determine *for all time* who I am – even if I do not believe in eternal life. From this point of view suicide could have an eternal meaning – disrobing me of any future possibility to give a different, more authentic expression of my true self.

Kierkegaard is right in observing that without a reference to eternity and transcendence it is hard to argue against a justification of suicide. "If from a pagan point of view one were to warn against self-slaughter, it must be by a long detour, by showing that it was breach of duty toward one's fellow-men" (1941, 73). Today's arguments against suicide are usually of this kind: suicide can inflict pain and suffering to our fellow humans, it represents a withdrawal from existing obligations (e.g. not fulfilling a promise) and other commitments (Stoecker 2006). However, Hume (2005) shows that the opposite can also be true: whoever commits suicide can disburden other people or alleviate their suffering. Without a transcendent authority, suicide can never be fully dismissed. Even Kant, who builds morality solely on reason and rejects any theological argumentation, condemns suicide by assuming the transcendent nature of reason itself (1993, 30-31). If there is no transcendent measure, if I am responsible only to me, than I can freely dispose of myself, including my own death. But the question remains of whether this apparent autonomy truly realises man's true self, or it is rather a state of his deep despair, as Kierkegaard would have considered it.

To conclude, we could say that it is not the physical act of self-killing which defines the phenomenon of suicide. Prior to this physical act there is a living *self*, which develops a particular and problematic understanding of its own self. It is in this lived understanding where a refusal of the self (self-negation) takes place, and from where the (act of) suicide originates. Besides this methodological shift, Kierkegaard reminds us that no understanding of the self can ultimately overcome the temptation of suicide unless it also acknowledges the transcendent Power which constituted it.

References

Anz, W. 1998: Kierkegaard on Death and Dying, in: J. Rée and J. Chamberlain (eds.), *Kierkegaard: A Critical Reader*, Oxford: Blackwell, pp. 39–52.

Derrida, J. 1995: *The Gift of Death*, Chicago: The University of Chicago Press.

Heidegger, M. 1986: *Sein und Zeit*, 16th ed., Tübingen: Niemeyer.

Hume, D. 2005: *Of Suicide*, New York: Penguin.

Kant, I. 1993: *Grounding for the Metaphysics of Morals*, 3rd ed., Indianapolis: Hackett.

Kierkegaard, S. 1941: *The Sickness Unto Death*, Princeton: Princeton University Press.

Ricoeur, P. 1998: Philosophy after Kierkegaard, in: J. Rée and J. Chamberlain (eds.), *Kierkegaard: A Critical Reader*, Oxford: Blackwell, pp. 9-25.

Seneca, L. A. 1999: *Philosophische Schriften*, 4th vol., Darmstadt: WBG.

Stoecker, R. 2006: Ein wirklich ernstes philosophisches Problem: Philosophische Reflexionen über den Suizid, in: *Zeitschrift für Bürgerrechte und Gesellschaftspolitik* 45: 4-23.

Wesche, T. 2003: *Kierkegaard: Eine philosophische Einführung*, Stuttgart: Reclam.

SUICIDE AND GENOCIDE IN THE LIGHT OF GIRARD'S MIMETIC THEORY

Robert Petkovšek, *Ljubljana*

Konrad Lorenz, Austrian zoologist and ethologist, and a Nobel laureate in physiology and medicine (1973), wrote in his book *On Aggression* that an extra-terrestrial being coming to the Earth would be astounded by the irrationality of human behavior. Humans are "jeopardized creatures," because the fruit that Adam and Eve picked from the tree of knowledge was not ripe (Lorenz 1966, 230). Human knowledge, based on man's capacity of using symbols, is a double-edged sword. On one hand, it enables man to transcend animal nature and to follow moral values; on the other hand, it makes him boundlessly aggressive. Humans are the only species capable of destroying itself. To illustrate this, Lorenz recalls the "Peking Man, the Prometheus who learned to preserve fire, used it to roast his brothers; beside the first traces of the regular use of fire lie the mutilated and roasted bones of *Sinanthropus pekinensis* himself" (231). In contrast to the animals, human being is an auto-aggressive being.

1. Archaic culture is dominated by mimetic desire

According to René Girard, human culture originates in mimetic desire. This raises the question, "What is mimetic desire?"

Firstly, desire creates man (Girard 2004, 9). To desire is to imitate; to imitate is to "become like". Imitation issues from desire, and desire issues from imitation. This is what Girard calls "mimetic desire". Aristotle believes that all animals imitate (*Poetics*, 48b6–7) but human beings imitate more than the animals; man is not just a mimetic being but a hyper-mimetic being. This makes him different from animals and raises him to the level of a transcendent, symbolic being.

What is "mimetic desire"? One desires another's objects or qualities; e.g., a student desires his teacher's knowledge. We believe that one desires the others' objects. As a matter of fact, we desire the objects because our models possess them. Essentially, we imitate our models; more precisely, we imitate what they desire. Our desires imitate our models' desires; finally, a desire desires a desire. This is how an apprentice learns. Once the imitator advances in learning he becomes in turn a model for his model so that the model starts imitating his imitator; the teacher imitates his apprentice. Thus, mutual imitation opens the door to competition and rivalry, and rivalry leads to conflicts, which increasingly spread out.

Mimetic desire thereby creates aggressiveness, which is intensified by revenge. Revenge means that aggressiveness is returned by even greater aggressiveness. Violence thus increases exponentially and transforms the community into a pot of violence. Once the community faces the threat of drowning in its own violence, a mechanism called "scapegoat" is triggered, whereby universal violence of all against all focuses on a single innocent victim. This polarization – known as "lynch" – changes into persecution and sacrifice of the innocent victim; the sacrifice returns reconciliation, peace and order to the community. Therefore, mimetic desire survives due to an innocent victim sacrificed as a scapegoat.

In a "mimetic cycle" universal mimetic violence issued from mimetic desire is redirected into ritual violence polarized on a single victim, whose innocence is disguised by myths. According to Girard, myths are created to conceal mimetic violence by deceptive narratives. Mimetic desire creates human culture but also menaces to destroy it because it fundamentally conveys exclusion and murder by first creating universal violence, which ends up in scapegoating, i.e. in ritual violence. So, archaic, pre-Christic culture is governed by hyper-mimetic desire, which encompasses the community like a fate that cannot be escaped.

2. Freedom born on the Cross

In the midst of archaic culture the event of the Cross was unpredictable and unexpected, in short, impossible. Sacrificed as a scapegoat on the Cross, Jesus did not react in accordance with the mimetic nature of man, i.e. with revenge, hatred, or curse, but with forgiveness that he asked the Father for his persecutors. Christ's prayer cannot be explained anthropologically from the viewpoint of mimetic desire, which constitutes human nature. To the contrary, the event takes its roots in revelation.

Philosophers like Jacques Derrida (2001, 31–2), Hannah Arendt (1958, 237), Paul Ricoeur (2000, 606) and others believe that modern global society has its origins in the forgiveness *discovered* by Christ on the Cross. Derrida and Ricœur explain globalization as globa-*latinization*. They insist that globalized world reflects the message of forgiveness brought to non-Christian peoples by the missionary work of the *Latin* Roman Catholic Church. Thereby, archaic culture of exclusion based on scapegoating has been gradually substituted by a new Christic culture of inclusion based on forgiveness.

Another fundamental element revealed on the Cross is the truth about the innocence of the scapegoat victims, which deprived ritual sacrifice of the almighty power that held archaic society together. Scapegoat victims have since been no longer unanimously believed guilty. Concern for innocent victims is considered the most important achievement of contemporary society; this concern, which subverted archaic ritual institutions, has changed the course of human history.

The event of the Cross is the birthplace of a new man, who was given the "law of liberty" as a new way of being and freedom as a new essence reborn from Christ. The "law of liberty" (James 1:25) has progressively leavened human society and has resulted in promotion of unselfish love. Put differently, revenge has progressively been overcome by forgiveness, in which contemporary globalized culture originates. However, the freedom originating in the "law of liberty" has developed in two opposite ways, as manifested by existential philosophy.

3. Existential thought as reflection of human freedom

Existential thought aims at thinking human existential freedom as radically experienced by Christ on the Cross. This experience has laid the foundation for a new culture that Girard calls "Christic" by contrast to pre-Christic, archaic culture, in which existential freedom had not yet been known. The "Law of liberty" given on the Cross opened two possible ways of applying existential freedom: an atheistic, Promethean way and a mystical, Marian way.

3.1 Atheistic Promethean existentialism

Philosophically, the idea of absolute human freedom was elaborated by Jean-Paul Sartre in his lecture 'Existentialism is a Humanism' (1952 [1946]), where he explains that in humans "existence precedes essence" (17). Existence is uniquely determined by man's own will. "Man is nothing else but what he purposes, he exists only in so far as he realizes himself, he is therefore nothing else but the sum of his actions, nothing else but what his life is" (44). "In other words, there is no determinism – man *is* free, man is freedom" (37). Sartre's existentialism is the kind of ontology of freedom that cannot be determined by any other instance. Therefore, God has to be removed from the horizon of human life. "We remind man that there is no legislator but himself; that he himself, thus abandoned, must decide for himself" (93).

The idea of absolute human freedom echoes the story of Adam and Eve, who saw God as their rival. This exclusive relationship may be explained in the light of mimetic desire: the imitator is attracted by his model but ends up in rivalry with the model. The idea of human freedom based on excluding the other is but a transformed archaic practice of scapegoating, which consists of expelling innocent victims. Sartre confirms this basic relationship in his drama *No Exit*, "Hell is – other people!"

In his talk Sartre refers to Dostoevsky whose thought he summarizes in the words, "if God did not exist, everything would be permitted" (36). As believed by Dostoevsky, exclusive freedom, which rises against God, leads to a total unleashing of violence. At the time when Russia was sinking into anarchism, nihilism, utilitarianism and atheism, Dostoevsky foresaw cultural decline already inaugurated by the fact that freedom had no longer resisted man's hypermimetism. Man wanted unlimited freedom for himself also with regard to God, as portrayed in *The Possessed*, where Dostoevsky described Kirillov's rivalry with God. Kirillov was ready to do anything just to demonstrate that his will is absolutely free and independent. Kirillov believed that absolute freedom might be best proved by suicide, which Kirillov also committed for this reason. He believed that committing suicide would show one had no fear of God because his will was greater than that of God. One's will is therefore ultimate reality, which is in consequence divine. "The attribute of my godhead is self-will." (*The Possessed,* Part III, Chap. 6, 2) This conclusion can be extended to the problem of relationship with other people. If there is no God, there is consequently nothing after death, and if so, there is no reason to act justly and morally. In his letter to Osmidov, Dostoevsky wrote, "If there is no immortality, I need but live out my appointed day, and let the rest go hang. And if that's really so (and if I am clever enough not to let myself be caught by standing laws), why should I not kill, rob, steal, or at any rate live at the expense of the others" (1961, 234).

In the historical situation Dostoevsky was analyzing, freedom was already showing up as a "new terrible freedom", subject to hyper-mimetic desire and no longer restrained by the scapegoat mechanism. He saw this "new terrible freedom" might give birth to an epidemic of genocides and suicides in the 20th century, resulting from violence of apocalyptic proportions.

3.2 Mystical or Marian existentialism

A different and diametrically opposite way of understanding existential freedom may be found in Martin Heidegger's conception of *Gelassenheit*, a concept borrowed from Meister Eckhart. For Heidegger, *Gelassenheit* means "the spirit of *disponibility* before What-Is which permits us simply to let things be in whatever may be their uncertainty and their mystery" (Heidegger 1959). The latter Heidegger conceived existence as dispossession (Ger. *Enteignis*), as not belonging to oneself but to the Being. Existence in this sense is not exclusive but inclusive. This is a philosophical transformation of the Eckhartian theological idea of the faithful's dispossession in God's presence, inspired by the event of the Cross, or more precisely, by Christ's renouncement of his own will in order to embrace the Father's will. In Christic sense, dispossession does not mean eradication of oneself but one's readiness to renounce one's own will so as to let oneself be placed in a state of total self-giving: the Cross. This enables one to hear the Father's word in his innermost being. Eckhart explains the concept of *Gelassenheit* as follows:

> "'Be asleep to all things': this means ignore time, creatures, images… And then you could perceive what God works in you. That is why the soul says in the Song of Songs, 'I sleep but my heart watches' (Sg. 5:2) Therefore, if all creatures are asleep in you, you can perceive what God works in you." (Eckhart 1993, 341 [Predigt 30, Praedica verbum])

The Eckhartian concept of *Gelassenheit* summarizes the tradition flowing from Christ's words on the Cross, "Let your will be done!" that the Holy Mother embraced in her readiness to live God's will, as expressed in her attitude of "*hu-*

militas animi" and in her words "*Fiat mihi secundum verbum tuum.*" In the liturgy, this basic attitude is expressed in the word "Amen".

3.3 Opposite ways of human freedom

Once the Cross divested archaic religion of its power, a new form of thinking – "existential thinking" – emerged, which is able to see man as an essentially free being, as a person or as an individual, whose desires are autonomous and decisions independent. The object proper to existential thinking is the "law of liberty" established on the Cross. Christic culture is therefore a form of human spirit that enables man to freely decide for himself and his future. The way of using this freedom determines the future: following the model of Jesus Christ, who renounced mimetic desire, leads to a new humanity and life, whereas following mimetic desire leads to the kind of freedom that becomes a starting point for increasing violence.

4. Genocide and suicide as prefiguration of apocalyptic violence

Since the foundation of human culture has man been exposed to the threat of violence generated by human hyper-mimetism. Human culture developed thanks to mimetic violence, which was regulated in archaic society by the scapegoat mechanism, i.e. by ritual violence, whose role was to eliminate excessive violence from the community. Archaic communities were protected from being drowned in their own violence by ritual violence, the role of which was to transfer the guilt for universal violence onto innocent victims.

On the Cross, ritual sacrifice was divested of the power that held archaic societies together. Jesus renounced the negative, scandalous mimetism that results in scapegoating. A consequence of Jesus' renouncement was a decline of archaic religion based on ritual violence, of which the original function was to restrain violence from escalating to the extremes that would lead to self-destruction of the community. The tendency toward escalation of violence is "natural elemental law" (Clausewitz 2000, part 3,16) of human mimetic nature. By renouncing it, Jesus became "foolishness to Gentiles" (1 Cor. 1:23). Christ's renouncement of revenge is unexplainable from the viewpoint of the "natural elemental law," which shows how the Cross brought radical novelty to human history. This prepared the way for love and forgiveness to become the basis of a new future, of "a new heaven and a new earth" (Rev 21:1). The Cross revealed that in the innermost part of his being Jesus was freedom itself, and that following Christ meant taking root in the freedom gained on the Cross.

According to Girard, the Cross is the generator and warrant of human existential freedom. This freedom is absolute with regard to human nature and its hypermimetism, which constitutes the "elemental law" of human nature. However, this freedom is a double-edged sword. The example of Jesus shows that – inasmuch as sustained by God – one may overcome the "natural elemental law", which leads to violence. On the other hand, by liberating humankind from ritual sacrifice this freedom exposes it to unleashed, unlimited violence, which tends to escalate to extremes. In *The Possessed* (part 3,6,2), Dostoevsky called it "terrible freedom," for it was by virtue of this freedom that Kirillov committed suicide, in order to demonstrate man's absolute freedom. Terrible freedom arises when mimetic violence is no longer under control. Absolute existential freedom born on the Cross may therefore be used in two ways; one may transform it by following the example of Jesus into a place of love and forgiveness, whereas one also may transform it by following negative mimetism into a place of unleashed and extreme forms of violence that may end up in an epidemic of either suicides or genocides, prefiguring the possibility of apocalyptic destruction of the world.

Girard believes mimetic violence is epitomized in the Bible by the name "Satan". Vis-à-vis the Cross, Satan – i.e., negative mimetism – was not able to achieve his genial strategy he had been uncompromisingly pursuing since the foundation of the world. Orthodox theology sees that, vis-à-vis the Cross, Satan failed for good. Since the event of the Cross, the "satanic mechanism" no longer has the capacity to master human destiny, because the violence and lie generated by this mechanism were dismantled on the Cross. The scapegoat mechanism has subsequently lost its efficiency, and mimetic violence has lost control over itself. The scapegoat mechanism was inherent to mimetic violence itself, the role of which was to restrain the violence from its tendency toward extremes. It was replaced by the twofold alternative, which clearly appears today, either renouncement of negative mechanism or escalation of violence toward extremes. These alternatives are due to the breakdown of the scapegoat mechanism and the consequent loss of the deceptive power of mythologies that held the scapegoat responsible for universal violence. Apocalyptic imagination depicting unlimited violence represents the utmost development of mimetic violence, which has no longer been controlled by the scapegoat mechanism. In contrast, Christic culture deeply believes that apocalyptic destruction may be avoided only through love and forgiveness.

Christ's renouncement of violence originates in his loyalty to the Father's will. His freedom flows from the Father's will. Loyalty to God's will enables one for a full development of positive freedom, whereas disloyalty leads to self-destruction, as shown in Chapter 12 and 20 of the Book of Revelation, which describe Satan's fall, "And the great dragon was cast out, that old serpent, called the Devil, and Satan, which deceiveth the whole world: he was cast out into the earth, and his angels were cast out with him" (Rev 12:9). Satan is under control for a "thousand years"; "after that he must be loosed a little season" (Rev 20:3). In his vision John predicts, "Woe to the inhabiters of the earth and of the sea! For the devil is come down unto you, having great wrath, because he knoweth that he hath but a short time" (Rev 12:12).

John the Evangelist recognized the agony on the part of Satan under the Cross as he was not able to overpower Jesus Christ. Consequently, Satan lost control over himself, which has made escalation of violence toward extremes a real possibility. The Cross became a symbol of the truth subverting the untruth generated by the violence. Once having faced the truth of its own untruth, satanic mimetic mechanism has no longer been able to control itself; awareness of its untruth has unleashed its rage such that no counter-weight may dampen its hyper-mimetic power except the renouncement of violence, as demonstrated by Jesus Christ.

To summarize, the destiny of humanity now depends on whether freedom is used in an atheistic Promethean way or in a mystical Marian way; it depends on man opting either for violence or for love. Freedom faces a fundamental alternative: either letting oneself go to extremes by mimetic violence or renouncing it. Jesus embraced the Cross because he found in love and forgiveness, concentrated on the Cross, the way out of the vicious circle of violence and revenge. Unfortunately, Dostoevsky prophetically foresaw that Western culture would embrace the other, opposite way – the way of exclusion as inaugurated by the rivalry of Eve and Adam with God, as represented by Kirillov in *The Possessed*, and as defended by Sartre in his atheistic existentialism.

The epidemic of suicide and genocide ravaging the contemporary world originates in "terrible freedom". Modern culture believes it can establish itself on unrestricted freedom. God has given man existential freedom, which liberates man in his innermost being and promotes him to the freedom of God's children. Thereby, man was given dignity in its fullness. However, the gift offered to humankind by Christ Crucified presupposes a new spiritual quality of humankind. As manifested in the most recent centuries, modern culture has been able to transform this freedom not into a place of love and forgiveness but, to the contrary, into a place of rivalry, exclusion, wars, extermination, genocides, that push to the frontiers of apocalypse. Within our culture, radical destruction is thus no longer impossible.

As a matter of fact, the movement of radical destruction is basically an oscillation between the possibility of universal destruction such as genocide on one hand and the possibility of self-destruction such as suicide on the other hand. This oscillation has the same root, which lies at the deepest level of human being, i.e., man's rivalry with God as diagnosed in the days of yore in the narrative of Adam and Eve.

The experience of absolute freedom claimed by Sartre is the freedom that Jesus was originally given on the Cross. Jesus' renouncement of mimetic desire opened the space for a new culture that has not ceased to deepen and expand in order to spread this freedom as its fundamental project. Jesus was able to renounce violence through his total loyalty to the Father's will. In philosophical terms, Meister Eckhart described Jesus' loyalty as "letting-be" (Ger. *Gelassen-*

heit). This attitude is the only alternative to the absolute and apocalyptic violence anticipated by the modern epidemic of genocides and suicides, which both result from the illusion that man is able to divinize himself. The antidote to full-fledged violence is the example of Jesus Christ, which paves the way to a new humanity reborn from renouncement of negative mimetism.

References

Alvarez, Al. 1972. *The Savage God: A Study of Suicide*. New York: Random House.
Arendt, Hannah. 1958. *The Human Condition*. Chicago: University of Chicago Press.
Clausewitz, Karl von. 2000 [1832]. *Vom Kriege*. München: Cormoran.
Derrida, Jacques. 2001. *On Cosmopolitanism and Forgiveness*. London: Routledge.
Dostoevsky, Fyodor Michailovitch. 1961. *Letters of Fyodor Michailovitch Dostoevsky to his Family and Friends*. New York: Horizon Press.
– – –. 2005. *The Possessed*. New York, NY: Barnes & Noble Classics.
Eckhart, Meister. 1993. *Werke*. Vol. 1, *Predigten*. Niklaus Largier, ed. Frankfurt am Main: Deutscher Klassiker Verlag.
Gans, Eric Lawrence. 1993. *Originary Thinking: Elements of Generative Anthropology*. Stanford, Calif.: Stanford University Press.
Girard, René. 1982. *Le bouc émissaire*. Paris: B. Grasset.
– – –. 1999. *Je vois Satan tomber comme l'éclair*. Paris: Grasset.
– – –. 2004. *Les origines de la culture*. Entretiens avec Pierpaolo Antonello and João Cezar de Castro Rocha. Paris: Desclée de Brouwer.
– – –. 2007. *Achever Clausewitz*. Entretiens avec Benoît Chantre. Paris: Carnets nord.
Heidegger, Martin. 1959. *Gelassenheit*. 2. ed. Pfullingen: Neske.
Lorenz, Konrad. 1966. *On Aggression*. London: Methuen.
McGrath, Alister. 2004. *The Twilight of Atheism: The Rise and Fall of Disbelief in the Modern World*. New York: Doubleday.
Ricœur, Paul. 2000. *La mémoire, l'histoire, l'oubli*. Paris: Seuil.
Sartre, Jean-Paul. 1952. *L'existentialisme est un humanisme* [1946]. Paris: Nagel.

ON THE CONCEPT OF GENOCIDE FROM THE POINT OF VIEW OF GROUPS AND HARM

Vojko Strahovnik, *Ljubljana*

Introduction: Definition of Genocide

Genocide is one of the darkest chapters in the history of humanity that has claimed many tens of millions deaths in the previous century only. Although it has been much investigated its comprehensive nature still seems to elude us. This paper is an attempt to shed some light on the concept and phenomenon of genocide from the point of view of groups, their value and the harm involved. The concept of genocide is controversial. A proper understanding of genocide is extremely important, even though the prospects of changing the accepted definition of genocide in international law and in legal practice seem bleak to begin with. An extended and deepened understanding of the concept of genocide can bring us closer to answers to several important questions regarding e.g. the recognition of genocide and genocidal acts, the foundations for our rejecting and condemnating genocide, and establishing (individual or collective) responsibility for genocide.

The paper thus focuses on our definition and understanding of the concept of genocide, with particular reference to two important dimensions that lay in the background of such an understanding. The first dimension is the dimension of *group(s)*, since genocide is understood as a crime committed against a group, and is on the other hand most often also a "collective" crime perpetrated by a group. This dimension of group(s) opens up a set of important questions, among which we can identify those that relate to the value of groups, to responsibility of individuals as members of a group or group agent, as well as those related to the responsibility of the group as a whole. The second dimension is the dimension of the *harm* involved in genocide – as closely connected to the mentioned value of the group that is targeted – and further related questions about the uniqueness of the crime of genocide and about our determination and understanding of this harm that justifies us to speak about genocide as "the crime of all crimes".

The concept of genocide has been initially developed by Polish lawyer Raphael Lemkin, when he – based on his reflection on the Nazi genocidal and occupation practices before and during the Second World War – pointed out the importance of this phenomenon and the necessary sanctions against it in the international law (1944, 90), since he saw it as one of the darkest sides of the history of mankind, a crime of barbarity, a crime against humanity, and the clearest case of breach of international law. After the end of the war, UN formulated a more definite formulation that has served also as a basis for *The Convention on the Prevention and Punishment of the Crime of Genocide (CG)* in 1948. This important document defines genocide as an act of intentional destruction of a national, ethnical, racial, or religious group (in whole or in part), including acts such as killing its members, causing them serious bodily or mental harm, prevention of birth, etc., while the types of acts punishable include genocide, conspiracy to commit genocide, direct and public incitement to commit genocide, attempt to commit genocide, and complicity in genocide (*CG*, Art. 2 and 3).

This definition is quite complex but the same time fairly definite regarding the supposed targets or types of groups that are recognized as relevant. As a prosecutable and punishable crime it involves two aspects, namely (i) *mens rea,* i.e. psychological or mental aspect or intention, which is in the case an intention to (in part or in whole) destroy a given group and (ii) *actus reus*, which is a physical aspect of this crime comprised of acts that lead or may lead towards such a destruction of a group (May 2009, 99–114). At the same time it must be emphasized that the fact that genocide as a crime is directed against a group (or against individuals as members of a group) is not the sole distinguishing characteristic of genocide, since similarly groups as such could be targets of crimes against humanity (in a narrow, legal sense), e.g. persecution against an identifiable group (*Rome Statute of the International Criminal Court*, Art. 7). The distinguishing characteristic is exactly the intention of and attempt of the destruction of a group (while with crimes against humanity the goals is usually to target individuals though possibly on a large scale) and corresponding harm and damage that can be suffered by individuals as victims based on their membership in the group.

Harm of Genocide and the Value of Groups

What are the distinctive values of groups that justify their special protection? What is the damage or harm involved in genocide to the group or individuals as members of a group (over and above the harm they suffer on the individual level)? Why is genocide as a crime against humanity so special and in which sense does it pose a threat to a common humanity? The question about the *value* of the group, against which the crime of genocide might be committed, and the question about the *harm* to the group or individuals as members of the group that this crime causes or results in, are independent of each other, but we can nevertheless consider them together since the usual approach takes the harm involved in genocide as precisely attacking the value of the group.

There are roughly two groups of answers to these questions. The first emphasizes the harm to an individual and the loss of value in regard to her membership in the group that offered her e.g. some type of protection or providing her with an opportunity of identification and making sense of her life. What is at stake here is a sort of harm to the individual, which gets inflicted to her with acts aimed towards a group, which member she is, or the so-called "status harm". In this regard we can speak about instrumental value of groups that can become targets of genocide. The second group of answers on the other hand emphasizes intrinsic or inherent value of the group itself, the destruction of which represents a loss of value for humanity. These two kinds of answers are of course not exclusive, so one can defend a sort of a hybrid view combining elements of both views. The first approach builds upon *instrumental* value of a group and a invokes *collective* conception of a group: the value of the group consists primarily in the group serving some interests of its members like protecting their rights, offering essential services, providing goods, or a sense of identity. The second approach builds upon *intrinsic* value of a group and invokes a *corporate* conception of a group: the value of the group is intrinsic and thus independent of the interest or needs of its members; the very existence of the group is therefore valuable (Kukathas 2011; Benhabib 2011).

The thought of Hannah Arendt offers us a profound insight into both types of view, since we can follow the development of her thought as moving from the first type to a position that also encompasses the second. In her *Origins of Totalitarianism,* based upon the immediate experience of totalitarian systems and the related genocidal acts, Arendt clearly states that the organization of Europe after the First World War created minorities that posed as easy targets of genocidal persecution, "stateless people", "scum of the earth", "undesirable", "unidentifiable beggars, without nationality, without money and without passports" (Arendt 1962, 269), to which the supposedly inalienable basic human rights were denied. What emerged was a form of "organized solitude" and isolation. The role, function or value of a (in this case national) group is that it offers an effective protection of individual's rights. "The second World War and the DP [displaced-persons, n. VS] camps were not necessary to show that the only practical substitute for a nonexistent homeland was an internment camp. Indeed, as early as the thirties this was the only 'country' the world had to offer the stateless" (Arendt 1962, 284). The value of the group is first and foremost in that it offers protection (legal or statutory) to an individual, which is related to the basic right, i.e. "the right to have rights", which represents a right of every human being to be recognized by others (and recognize others in turn) as a person entitled to moral respect and legally protected rights on the basis of common humanity (Benhabib 2011, 59–60).

Similarly Claudia Card (2003) sees genocide as a form of social death. The damage and harm suffered by the victims of genocide is social death – the loss of social vitality, liveliness and identity related to the meaningfulness of life. Genocide does not necessarily include mass killing or total annihilation of a given group, though such killing is often associated with it. With genocide we are dealing with an evil and a crime that goes beyond mere injustice, since the victims suffer harm that "makes victims' lives unbearable, indecent, or impossible, or that make victims' deaths indecent" (Card 2003, 66). The loss of social vitality emerges out of a permanent and irreversible destruction of social ties, i.e. social organization, practices, and institutions. This impacts and threatens the vital interests of the victims even before their possible physical death and in this way robs them of the meaning and any kind of control over their lives. Social death means the loss of the meaning of life and also makes the death of the victims meaningless. In order to show that the damage and evil of genocide is something that cannot be reduced to the damage or loss that can in any other way inflict an individual as a victim of e.g. war crimes or other crimes against humanity, we must link this damage and loss with the intention to destroy the group as such. Social death is the characteristic that enables us to do so as specific for genocide, since in other crimes against humanity or war crimes it is evident that individuals can become victims independently of their membership in a group (Card 2003, 77). From this it also follows that the crime of genocide cannot be exclusively connected solely with the destruction of a national, ethnical, racial, or religious group, but instead that we must include any other type or token of a group, whose destruction can bring about social death of its members. Likewise Žalec (2013) shows that such an extended definition of genocide is necessary, that genocide is a morally laden concept and it further elaborates its understanding in relation to concepts phenomena of humanity, totalitarianism and terrorism. Juhant (2013) emphasises social exclusion from the community of humanity as a pathway to genocide, since such exclusion paves way for social death (and individual's physical death).

Larry May (2003) also develops the view that builds upon instrumental value of groups. The harm involved in genocide is status harm, which befalls an individual when the group is targeted and attacked. First, there is an aspect of individual's identity, which is tied to the group and through which she is identified and recognized in society. Secondly, this identity as linked to a group is an important part of individual's own understanding of her history and place in society. And thirdly, a group often plays a role of a protector of interests and right of an individual; an attack on the group is an attack on this bulwark. A group therefore in many cases represents a final haven for the protection of individual's basic human rights and at the same time provides an important aspect of her identity and meaning. Genocide as a crime against such a group endangers, abates or even destroys both of these aspects. The crime of genocide is not first and foremost a crime that would harm a group, but it harms individuals as members. A group has no inherent value; its value is merely instrumental from the point of view of members of the group (May 2009, 75). Similarly, proposal leads to the extension of the concept of genocide to include any group, the destruction of which can lead to the mentioned kind of harm to an individual. All the so far presented views about the harm of genocide are quite similar to each other in this regard.

This second kind of answer to our initial question goes into the direction of understanding the harm of genocide as a loss of value for humanity, when a group is destroyed or endangered. Given one of the possible interpretations the loss of value emerges out of the loss of contribution that a given group could bring for humanity and its development. But one must note that is probably not sensible to understand this as some sort of simple model of value of diversity (as it is the case with development of species and biotic diversity), where diversity itself is the only evaluative dimension. At most we can understand such loss and harm for humanity in an indirect manner. This type of approach is present in Arendt, especially in her works that followed *The Origins of Totalitarianism*, when she moved away from her initial scepticism about the effectiveness of international law and human rights (cf. Arendt 1962, 292) and is also taking into account the shift from radical evil to the banality of evil perspective. Arendt develops an understanding of genocide as a crime against humanity (in the widest sense of the term) and a crime without precedent, as it was characterized by the *Charter of the International Military Tribunal* before the Nuremberg trials (8. 8. 1945). As such genocide as a crime is independent of the state of war. In her book *Eichmann in Jerusalem* Arendt states that one can understand a crime that Eichmann was trialed for as if "extermination of whole ethnic groups – the Jews, or the Poles, or the Gypsies – might be more than a crime against the Jewish or the Polish or the Gypsy people" and due to which "that the international order, and mankind in its entirety, might have been grievously hurt and endangered" (Arendt 1977). Genocide is a crime that endangers the human status itself, a crime "against human nature", without which the meaning of humanity and human dignity is completely empty; we are dealing with "an attack upon human diversity as such" (Arendt 1977). "It is because we inhabit a world with others who are like us yet always different from us that the world is perspectivical and can only manifest itself to us from a particular vantage point" (Benhabib 2011, 46-47). Plurality enables diversity and perspectivity. As such is in its essence different from e.g. persecution or pogroms of Jews, since Holocaust as genocide only took over from anti-Semitism the selection of victims but not the essence of the crime itself. Genocide violates "the order of mankind" and cannot be compared to e.g. murder (Arendt 1977).

A similar justification of the uniqueness of the crime of genocide is put forward by Lemkin, who sees genocide as a crime of barbarity. It is targeted against a group as such and its destruction represent the loss of value for humanity. "The world represents only so much culture and intellectual vigor as are created by its component national groups. [...] The destruction of a nation, therefore, results in the loss of its future contributions to the world" (Lemkin 1944, 91). As such these groups are discovered, not created. But such understanding of the uniqueness of the crime of genocide is burdened by several open questions. First, there is a rather vague definition of a nation and its relatedness to other kinds of groups mentioned as targets in the *CG*. Next, there is an open question, whether such understanding establishes some sort of hierarchy of national groups in relation to the scope of probable (if at all possible) contributions to mankind. And if the latter is the case, i.e. if a group that lacks such a potential is destroyed, can we still speak about genocide as the crime against humanity? And lastly, how do we understand minorities within a particular national group? We can see that Lemkin is still operating under the presupposition or framework of traditional account of nations and in the context of European historical experience, which prevents him to formulate a more suitable and coherent conception of genocide. Seyla Benhabib (2011, 46) thus convincingly argues that Lemkin's understanding of the ontology of groups and their value originates mainly from Wilson's points and category and status of minorities in them, and further back out of Herder's conception of national communities as bearers of cultural and artistic achievements of humanity. From this point of view Arendt's account is more prolific and flexible for different forms of the genocidal crimes, and at the same time does not understand particular groups as predetermined, unchangeable, and direct manufacturers of original contributions to humanity, but instead as phenomenal forms of human diversity and plurality, which open up different perspectives on the world and which we can freely form and transform as part of our human condition (Benhabib 2011, 51-54, Benhabib 1988, Arendt 2005, 175).

An Extended Definition of Genocide

Based on the considerations above regarding groups as targets of genocide, we can conclude with some ideas about a more suitable definition and understanding of the concept of genocide that would reach beyond its established delineation in international law.

It is necessary to extend the set of kinds of groups included in the concept of genocide. This should be done in a way to include all groups that can represent a fairly stable and robust identification for individuals and that can at the same time be seen as part and expression of the variety and plurality (in Arendt's sense). Irrespective of the preferred viewpoint on the nature and scope of damage and loss involved in genocide and the value of a group (instrumental or inherent) we cannot justify limiting genocide to kinds of groups currently explicitly mentioned in the *CG*. If one takes the collective/instrumental view of groups and their value, then any of the chosen instrumental values (protection of interest, sense of identity, protection of basic rights, social vitality, etc.) would place such a limited definition of genocide and protected groups in the following well-known dilemma. Either the criteria would be too strict and would thus fail to include every national, ethnical, racial, or religious group or if we set the criteria more broadly, then we will have to include many other groups. One would then have to propose a normative criterion that would secure the inclusion of only national, ethnical, racial, or religious groups and no other groups and nothing like this has been put forward so far. On the other hand, if one chooses to defend a corporate/intrinsic view of groups and their value the task is to put forward an argument that would demonstrate that all and only these kinds of group have intrinsic value and that all other groups lack it. We saw above how both Lemkin and Arendt struggle with this, since there is no in principle criteria that would limit the value of plurality, human diversity, and contribution to humankind only to these types of groups. Next, a physical destruction of a group is not a necessary condition of speaking about the crime of genocide; the latter encompasses all other acts, with which the mentioned harm or loss could be inflicted. What also poses a challenge is a more clear illumination of the aspect of intention and separation of it from a motive for action. This is further connected with the proposal to include considerations on group agents and responsibility of the members inside them that may have different roles; the responsibility rests not merely on the direct executors of those acts or planner of some explicit central plan for carrying out such atrocities, but to other members of group agent as well.

Such an extended understanding of the crime of genocide would allow us to more easily identify and persecute it successfully. At the same time we should follow an idea to discontinue regarding it as the "crime of all crimes", that is completely unique and significantly exceeds other crimes against humanity or war crimes, because this can raise the criteria for the adoption of measures by the international community and diminishes chances for such a crime to be (at least in some cases) prevented (cf. May 2009, 109; 130). A telling example is a report of the UN Secretariat on the situation in Rwanda in 1994, which at that time did not describe the events as genocide, although a more decisive intervention of the international community rather than the withdrawal of military peacekeepers could significantly mitigate the extent of already ongoing genocide. The assessment of the UN on the situation Darfur was similar, since the events were originally described as war crimes and crimes against humanity, but not as genocide. All this is the result of over-rigid definition of genocide and related deeply rooted considerations about the uniqueness of this crime.

References

Arendt, H. 1962. *The Origins of Totalitarianism.* New York: Meridian books.

Arendt, H. 1977. *Eichmann in Jerusalem.* New York: Penguin books.

Arendt, H. 2005. *The Promise of Politics.* New York: Schocken Books.

Benhabib, S. 1988. Judgment and the Moral Foundations of Politics in Arendt's Thought. *Political Theory* 16(1), 29–51.

Benhabib, S. 2011. *Dignity in Adversity. Human Right in Troubled Times.* Cambridge: Polity.

Card, C. 2003. Genocide and Social Death. *Hypatia* 18(1), 63–79.

Charter of the International Military Tribunal. 1945. http://law2.umkc.edu/faculty/projects/trials/nuremberg/NurembergIndictments.html; accessed 16. 2. 2013.

Convention on the Prevention and Punishment of the Crime of Genocide (CG). 1948. Paris, 9 December 1948, available at: http://treaties.un.org/doc/Publication/UNTS/Volume%2078/volume-78-I-1021-English.pdf; accessed 15. 9. 2013.

Juhant, J. 2013. Political Crime and the Truth of Man. The Slovene Case. *Anthropological Notebooks,* 19 (2), 7–24.

Kukathas, C. 2011. Review of *Genocide. A Normative Account* (Larry May). *Notre Dame Phil. Reviews*; available at: http://ndpr.nd.edu/news/25988-genocide-a-normative-account/; accessed 15. 9. 2013.

Lemkin, R. 1944. *Axis Rule in Occupied Europe: Laws of Occupation, Analysis of Government, Proposals for Redress.* Washington: Carnegie Endowment for International Peace.

May, L. 2010. *Genocide. A Normative Account.* New York: Cambridge UP.

Rome Statute of the International Criminal Court. 1998. available at: http://legal.un.org/icc/statute/romefra.htm; accessed 15. 9. 2013.

Žalec, B. 2013. Genocide as Social Death. A Comparative Conceptual Analysis. *Anthropological Notebooks,* 19 (2), 57–74.

BEYOND THE LEGAL DEFINITION OF GENOCIDE

Jernej Letnar Černič, *Kranj*

Human beings can in moments of dehumanisation, pride and arrogance cause unimaginable evil. Genocide represents the most radical and irrational evil, which many experts have often described as a "crime of crimes" (Schabas, 2009). Crime of genocide is "opposed to the moral law" (GA Res. 96 (I), UN Doc. A/64/Add.1 (11 December 1946). Effective prosecution of such crimes, therefore, plays a key role in the purification of individual and collective consciousness of the respective societies. The Supreme Court of Israel stated in *Eichmann* case that "no human pen, no human tongue can ever succeed in describing the barest outline of suffering of millions, who were killed, slaughtered and burned ..." (*Attorney General of Israel v. Eichmann*, 36 I.L.R. 277, 322) The legal definition of genocide does not have a long history. In the year before the end of the Second World War it was coined by Raphael Lemkin in his book "Axis Rule and Occupied Europe" (Lemkin, 1944). Although the Allies did not include crime of genocide in the *ratione materiae* of the International Military Tribunal in Nuremberg (Schabas, 2012, p. 108-111), Lemkin concluded that the "the evidence produced at the Nuremberg trial gave full support to the concept of genocide" (Lemkin, 1947, str. 147). The United Nations General Assembly later adopted on this basis the Resolution, and then the Convention on the Prevention and Punishment of Genocide, which Article 2 provides the definition of genocide. Crime of genocide is one of those heinous crimes where state can exercise universal jurisdiction, although Article 6 of the Convention only provides for territorial jurisdiction. The latter may be the lowest minimum, which, as noted by the Israeli court in the case of Eichmann "did not affect the existing jurisdiction of States under customary international law" (36 I.L.R. 5, 11 (Summary).

The legal definition of genocide is more or less clear. The Convention provides that genocide "means any of the (five) acts committed with intent, in whole or in part, a national, ethnical, racial or religious group, as such". Among the five acts definition includes the following actions, which are listed exhaustively: "(a) killing members of the group (b) causing serious bodily or mental harm to members of the group (c) deliberately inflicting on the group conditions of life calculated to bring about its full or partial physical destruction, (d) imposing measures intended to prevent births within the group, and (e) forcibly transferring children of the group to another group".

The latter activity may be directed only against one individual that does not need to be part of the widespread and systematic genocidal policy either of state or non-state entities. It relates to both physical and spiritual integrity of the individual or the protected groups. Killing members of protected groups includes the murder of individuals who belong to this group (Jelišić case, para. 63). Causing serious bodily or mental harm refers to both physical as well as psychological mutilation of members of protected groups that would threaten the existence of such a group (Kayishema and Ruzindana case, para. 113). The third act, deliberately inflicting on the group conditions of life calculated to bring about its full or partial physical destruction, refers to actions that are not directly oriented to the immediate killing members of the group. The latter offense includes inhuman living conditions, denial of medical assistance, water, food, clothing and footwear, education, forced and child labour and inhumane transports of people. Jurisprudence requires that the offense is committed against a group as such, even if only partially, while not sufficient that the act is directed against only one individual (Akayesu case, para. 505). The fourth act relates to acts intended to prevent births within the group, thereby causing "biological genocide" group (Jessberger, 2009, p. 101). The potential acts include rape, forced sterilization, forced marriages and ban on contraception. The fifth group is ban on forcibly transferring children of the group to another group, thereby destroying the language, culture and customs of the protected group. At this point, the Convention prohibits cultural genocide, which refers to the cultural destruction due to the forced migration or a direct threat to coerce descendants of one group to another group.

A key component of the definition of genocide is "the purpose of fully or partially destroy" one of the protected groups, whereas disagreements revolve mainly on the number and description of the protected groups. All genocidal actions must be executed with the specific intention. Full and partial destruction of the group must be previously part of the offender's plan (Jessberger, 2009, p. 106). Since it is difficult to prove specific intent, it can be deduced from circumstantial evidence such as nature, systematic actions targeting victims because of their membership of a protected group and the general circumstances of the crimes (*Jelišić* case, Appeals Chamber, para. 47). Motive of the perpetrator is not a requirement for the commission of crimes. There is no requirement that the perpetrator totally or partially destroys one of the protected groups, it is sufficient that it only intended only to partially destroy it (*Jelišić* case, Trial Chamber, para. 95). Latter condition is assessed quantitatively, and geographical position of individuals within the group, with the primary role of representing the consequences of the existence of the group (*Krstić* case, Trial Chamber, para. 595). If the perpetrators focus on the political and intellectual leaders of protected groups, such action falls within the prohibition of genocide, as this can destroy the top of the group. Of course, the act must be committed against the group as such and not just against an individual, which is a random member of a protected group. In other words, the target of the attack is the group, not the individual (*Jelišić* case, Trial Chamber, para. 79) deliberately inflicting on the group conditions of life calculated to bring about its full or partial physical destruction.

The international definition of genocide includes four protected groups: national, ethnical, racial or religious group. In practice, the courts have used several approaches in identifying whether a particular group of individuals belong to one of the protected groups. The most common are objective and subjective approaches. Objective approach argues that a group belongs to a protected group on the basis of objective circumstances, such as language, common history, culture and traditions. Subjective approach focuses on their own perception of the group. Each group has its own wish that it be defined as a specific group and be granted the appropriate regulatory protections. If the majority of potential members have not expressed an interest in incorporating them into some definitions or categories, such group does not arise or cease to exist.

The International Criminal Tribunal for Rwanda held in the *Akayesu* "that the crime of genocide was allegedly perceived as targeting only 'stable' groups, constituted in a permanent fashion; groups the membership of which is determined by birth, with the exclusion of the more 'mobile' groups which one joins through individual voluntary commitment, such as political and economic groups. Therefore, a common criterion in the four types of groups protected by the Genocide Convention is that membership of such groups would seem to be normally not challengeable by their members, who belong to it automatically, by birth, in a continuous and often irremediable manner" (*Akayesu*, Trial Chamber, para.511). Basis for the definition of a protected group is therefore membership in a permanent and protected group. The Court has thus adopted in the *Akayesu* an objective approach to the definition of protected groups, which derives from the fact of belonging as not only a consequence of the decision of the individual. Individuals become members of the group by birth, which means that this fact with the autonomy of their will cannot be changed in later life.

The International Criminal Court has distanced itself from an objective approach in the case of *Kayishema and Ruzindana*, where it stated that the "an ethnic group is one whose members share a common language and culture; or, a group which distinguishes itself, as such (self-identification); or a group identified as such by others, including perpetrators of the crimes (identification by others)" (para. 98). Membership of individuals in a particular depends on her decision, and not on any objective facts. Subjective characteristics must therefore be primarily present. The same court distanced itself from this approach in the *Rutaganda* case, where it noted that "the concepts of national, ethnic, racial, and religious groups had been researched extensively and that, at present, there are no generally and internationally accepted precise definitions thereof. Each of these concepts must be assessed in the light of a particular political, social, and cultural context" (Trial Chamber, para. 56). Under this decision either objective and subjective characteristics of a protected group must be present. There has been a shift from cumulative to an alternative approach. Thereafter, the International Tribunal for the Former Yugoslavia employed in the *Jelišić* case a subjective approach, as "using objective and scientifically irreproachable criteria would be a perilous exercise whose result would not necessarily correspond to the perception of the persons concerned by such categorisation" (*Jelesić*. Trial Chamber, para. 70). Subjective approach should be used on the basis of the positive and negative criteria for judging whether individuals belong to any of the protected groups (*Jelesić*, Trial Chamber, para. 70). Here it should be noted that genocide means use of violence in order to fully or partially destroy a national, ethnical, racial or religious group, as such. Also, the phrase "as such" requires that one of the overt acts of genocide directed also against a national, ethnical, racial or religious group. It is not sufficient that the act is directed against individuals who are not members of a particular group. The ICTY noted in *Stakić* case that: "Raphaël Lemkin explained that genocide constitutes such a serious offence in part because the world loses "future contributions" that would be "based upon [the destroyed group's] genuine traditions, genuine culture, and … well-developed national psychology." Thus, genocide was originally conceived of as the destruction of a race, tribe, nation, or other group with a particular positive identity – not as the destruction of various people lacking a distinct identity (Appeals Chamber, para. 21).

In defining protected groups one can differ between objective, subjective and mixed approaches. Nowadays, it is difficult to define which the definition of protected groups, objective, subjective, or mixed is universally accepted. Everything is dependent on subsequent decisions of international courts (Martin, 2009, 126-127). However, it seems that the mixed definition increasingly comes to the fore by including both objective and subjective approaches.

Commentators have for a long time pointed out that the Convention on the Prevention and Punishment of the Crime of Genocide defines "only a basic minimum" (Van Schaack, 1997, p. 2277), whereas customary international law may include also protected other groups outside the internationally protected categories. For example, Nersessian advocates for the inclusion of political groups in the international definition of genocide, from which they were released due to political pressure during the drafting of the Convention and notes that their exclusion from the definition of the Convention was "political compromise" (Nersessian, 2010, p. 111). The exclusion of political groups from the definition of genocide is often attributed to the pressure exercised by the delegation of the Soviet Union. While the latter is true, exclusion of political groups was also supported by a large coalition of countries from different geographical parts of the world (Schabas, 2009, 160). Finally, only those four groups were included in the definition for which there was agreement.

Some definitions of domestic jurisdictions include political and social groups. For instance, Article 100 (1) of the Criminal Code of the Republic of Slovenia provides for only four protected groups, while omitting political and social groups. Article 100 provides second paragraph that "the same punishment shall be imposed on whoever commits any of the acts under the previous paragraph against any group because of the reasons referred to in indent 8 of Article 101". The next provision, Article 101 of the Criminal Code (KZ-1), criminalizes crimes against humanity and provides in indent 8 that "persecution, which represents intentional or severe encroachment of fundamental rights contrary to the international law, against any identifiable group or community on political, racial, national, ethnic, cultural, religious, gender …".

The current regulation of the prohibition of genocide is in the Slovenian Criminal Code very unusual. If one defines the protected groups broadly, prosecutors could then prosecute genocide on the basis of Slovenian Criminal Code also against the political and social groups. If one takes a narrower approach, the first question is why the drafters of the Slovenian Criminal Code did not include political and social groups in the primary prohibition of genocide? In this way, it appears that the current Slovenian regulation of protected groups is not only uncommon, but also to be inadequate and inappropriate.

All in all, the legal definition of genocide is therefore composed of at least five elements: genocidal specific intent, genocidal offense, attack the victims because of their membership in a protected group, genocidal action should be part of the systematic and indiscriminate attacks and targeted at least partial destruction of a protected group.

Can a legal, sociological or any other definition of genocide capture all its dimensions from real life scenarios? The concept of genocide also has wider significance in the cultural, historical and media context, where all systematic human rights violations have been often classified as genocide. The question is whether this use of the word genocide can heal the emotional wounds of victims' relatives and society as a whole? The use of the word "genocide" has a special significance to relatives of the victims of genocide, since their loved ones were killed due to the realization of the maximum of evil in human society. Genocide has also a special importance for education of the younger generations about the most serious crimes. Various empirical studies have shown that the word genocide quickly establishes itself in the individual and collective memory.

Payam Akhavan notes that "judicial encounters with such radical evil thus provide a valuable glimpse into whether and how something so irrational and intensely emotional can be translated into the strictures of legal idiom" (Akhavan, 2012, p. 10).

The legal concept of genocide covers only a fraction of its dimension, which extends to the field of psychology through social sciences to forensic science, which is why the legal definition of genocide is equally limited as are limited its definitions in other scientific fields. The legal definition of genocide neglects and omits the emotional dimensions of such a crime, as it not only deals with its direct victims, but neglects the suffering of survivors, i.e. victims' relatives and future generations. Hannah Arendt raised this concern in a letter to Karl Jaspers when she noted that Nazi crimes "explode the limits of the law" (Arendt, 1992, p. 54).

The legal definition of genocide is often too narrow and many experts have been for many years wondering whether the criminal prosecutions of genocide even make any sense as it is very difficult to prove the specific intent required by the crime of genocide. Although there have been convictions of perpetrators of genocide before international and national criminal courts, its success and significance should be assessed in terms of its importance of education and catharsis of respective societies. The concept of genocide is much more than a mere legal definition, arising from domestic and international law. It consists mainly of support to relatives of victims and affected societies and enables them to clean themselves internally and externally on individual and collective level, to take the blame, create feelings of shame and lay the groundwork for the future on the basis of past mistakes, when individuals and societies were dehumanized.

References

Akhavan, Payam. *Reducing Genocide to Law*. Cambridge, Cambridge University Press, 2012.

Arendt, Hannah. *The Origins of Totalitarianism*. New York, Schocken books, 2004.

Kohler, Lotte & Saner, Hans (eds.). Letter to Karl Jaspers in *Hannah Arendt/Karl Jaspers : Correspondence 1926-1969,* trans. Robert Kimber and Rita Kimber. New York, Harcourt Brace Jovanovich, 1992, 51, 54, cited in Payam Akhavan, *Reducing Genocide to Law*. Cambridge, Cambridge University Press, 2012, p. 180.

Jessberger, Florian. The Definition and the Elements of the Crime of Genocide, pp. 87-111, in Paola Gaeta, *The UN Genocide Convention – A Commentary*. Oxford, Oxford University Press, 2009.

Lemkin, Raphael. *Axis Rule in Occupied Europe: Laws of Occupation, Analysis of Government, Proposals for Redress*. Washington, DC, Carnegie Endowment for World Peace, 1944.

Lemkin, Raphael. Genocide as a Crime Under International Law, 41 *American Journal of International Law 145*, 147 (1947).

Martin, Fanny. The notion of "protected group" in the Genocide convention and its application, 112-127 in Paola Gaeta, *The UN Genocide Convention – A Commentary*. Oxford, Oxford University Press, 2009.

Nersessian, David. *Genocide and Political Groups*. Oxford, Oxford University Press, 2010.

Van Schaack, Beth. Note, The Crime of Political Genocide: Repairing the Genocide Convention's Blind Spot, 106 *Yale Journal of International Law* 2259, 2277 (1997).

Schabas, William. *Genocide in International Law: The Crime of Crimes*. Cambridge, Cambridge University Press, 2009.

Schabas, William. *Unimaginable atrocities*. Oxford, Oxford University Press, 2012.

Sémelin, Jacques. *Očistiti in uničiti* [*Purifier et détruire*]. Ljubljana, *Mordijan*, 2009.

Judgment of domestic and international courts

Attorney General of Israel v. Eichmann, 36 I.L.R. 277, 322 (Supreme Court of Israel, 1962)

Prosecutor v. Georges Anderson Nderubumwe Rutaganda. ICTR-96-3-T, Trial Chamber Judgement, 6 December 1999.

Prosecutor v. Goran Jelesić. IT-95-10-T, Trial Chamber Judgement, 14 December 1999.

Prosecutor v. Jean-Paul Akayesu. ICTR-96-4-T, Trial Chamber Judgement, 2 September 1998.

SUICIDE AS A TOPIC OF THE ETHICAL THEORIES IN HUNGARIAN INTELLECTUAL HISTORY UNDER THE CONDITIONS OF THE POST-WAR MORAL CRISIS AFTER THE WWI

Béla Mester, *Budapest*

However, the problem of suicide is a continuous problem of the ethical theories from the beginning of the history of the moral philosophy it has usually just a secondary significance as an application of moral teaching in marginal occasions. An extreme moral case of suicide can have a central position in a discourse in the times of moral and cultural crises, connected to the turning points of the theories which interpret this situation. The texts of moral philosophy analysed below were written in 1921, in a typical situation of the post-war moral crisis. Experiences of the WWI have shocked the society, and provoked the common concepts of the human body and death. Killed humans and destroyed bodies have become a visible mass phenomenon for a significant number of people in forms never seen before: soldiers died of gas-attack, mass of veterans with amputated legs and hands, departments of psychiatry filled with soldiers suffering of new kinds of "neuroses of the frontiers."

In the same time, at least in the Hungarian case, there was a tension in the intellectual life, concerning the influence of the different answers for the moral crisis offered in the same time by the anthropologies of the positivism and the different tendencies of neo-idealisms. Significant figures of the Hungarian intellectual life have alienated from their ideals before the war that is the irrational tendencies of the *fin de siècle* "philosophies of life", accused of the preparation for the war-hysteria of the European societies.[1] In this situation, under circumstances of the post-war trauma and a special turning point of the philosophical life the inauguration lecture of a correspondent member of the Hungarian Academy of Sciences, Jenő Posch, focussed on the problem of the suicide, was published on the pages of the most significant Hungarian literary periodical, entitled *Nyugat (West)*; and has provoked a vivid debate. Suicide is not a usual topic for an academic inauguration lecture, and a literary periodical is not a usual forum for an academic paper; circumstances of publication mirrors the actuality of the question in the Hungarian thought of this time.

[1] A famous example of this intellectual trend is an essay of a significant figure of the Hungarian literature in the interwar period, Mihály Babits (1883–1941), entitled *A Dangerous Worldview* (Babits 1918). By the opinions of Babits, the anti-intellectual, irrational climate of the philosophies of the previous century had prepared the European thought for the war-hysteria.

The Intellectual Atmosphere

Nyugat (1908–1941) was the most influential centre of the Hungarian intellectual life for three generations; its chief editor was in the period of the debate *Mihály Babits.* Its spirit was highly sensitive for the post-war social, political and cultural trauma, as it is mirrored both on the pages of the periodical, and in the individual works of its main contributors in this time. It is known that it was one of the few of the significant, consequently pacifist periodicals on the Hungarian scene in the years of the war-hysteria. However, the shadow of the war is visible everywhere in the analysed texts; direct references to the war-facts are under a special psycho-social inhibition. For example, there is an important subtopic, the military self-sacrifice as a marginal case between a heroic and altruistic act and the suicide in its strict meaning. Instances of this important phenomenon come from the antiquity and from the national legendary of the Turkish wars, avoiding the war ended three years before. In the same time, the texts were penetrated by the indirect war-experiences, partly unconsciously. Suicide as the last remedy in the common thinking of this age appears in the metaphor of the "iron reserve," the last conserved meat in the bottom of the soldier's bag, which will be unmasked as an empty tin-box (*The Suicide from the point of View of the Psychology, and Ethics;* Posch 1921, 391).[2] A man after the amputation of his both legs in narcosis, and his experiences about his own body appears as a model of a painless suicide (*On Suicide;* Füst 1921, 468–469), and so on. Editors of the periodical have published a short cut selection of the discussion on the inauguration lecture. The only published opponent was *Milán Füst* (1888–1967), a significant contributor of the periodical. Füst's style and intellectual horizon was not far from the "philosophies of life," and in his articles he makes direct references to them. The main feature of his *œuvre* is a deep, precise psychical analysis of his characters, including the "dark side" of the psyche; and his personality was not free from psychical problems. In the time of the debate his book of collected poems entitled *Chorus of the Death* was prepared, published in the end of the same year, and several examples of this *poetical thanatology* were published in the days of the debate on the pages of the same periodical, with the same title (Füst 1921a, 1921b).

A Protagonist of the Debate on Suicide: Jenő Posch

The initiator of the debate on suicide, *Jenő* (in his publications in German: *Eugen*) *Posch (1859–1923)* has a special position in the Hungarian philosophical life. In his lifetime the main trend of the academic life was a turn from the ideas of positivism to the systems of neo-idealism, with an axiology and moral questions in its focus. The development of the thought of Posch followed a reciprocal way: in the early publications he focussed on the problem of time in the

---

[2] Posch for the "iron reserve" used here the German expression "eiserner Vorrat" within the Hungarian text, referring to the vocabulary of the Austro-Hungarian army.

Kantian conceptual framework (*A Theory of Time;* Posch 1896–1897), than he later developed a new theory of human being, rooted in positivist ideas, and was later recognised as the ancestor of the philosophical behaviourism (see McGuigan 1978). This unique way of the development of his thinking was connected with scandals: the discussion on his early main work on the concept of time touched the political life, several Parliamentary interpellations and Ministerial interventions happened in his case, and, in the end he officially declared his departure from the Catholic Church because of the differences of the concept of time in his own philosophy, and the official Catholic opinions. He never had a position on the universities. His entrance into the academic life and his distance from the university sphere have established the legend of an eccentric, solitary author in the margin of the intellectual life of his epoch. Actually he was always in the centre of cultural and academic life; his masters were central figures of the Hungarian philosophy; his articles were published on the pages of the best Hungarian academic and cultural periodicals of his epoch. Six years after the publication of his proto-behaviourist masterpiece (*Our Psychical Phenomena and Their Nature: A Plan for a Realist Psychology;* Posch 1915),[3] in 1921, he achieved the top of his academic career, the correspondent membership of the Hungarian Academy of Sciences, after the vice-presidency of the Hungarian Philosophical Society in a time when his thought was an odd one between the neo-idealist philosophies of his contemporaries, connected to conservative political ideas and circles. He chose the topic of the suicide as a psychical and ethical problem for his inauguration lecture in the Academy. That question had an actuality under conditions of the post-war moral crisis, and fitted to his program after his masterpiece which was a formulation of the *moral consequences* of his anthropology in details, from the question of the animal rights to the problem of suicide. Let us see the main concept of his anthropology before the detailed analyses of his opinions on suicide.

Theoretical background: an anti-metaphysical cleaning of the language

The main idea of his masterpiece is a systematic anti-metaphysical cleaning of the vocabulary of the philosophy of mind. In this critique of the language, the terms of 'soul' and 'mind' are in the centre of his target. Posch defines his position amongst the recent philosophical systems by his radical linguistic analysis of the obscure scholar and common words for human personality. By the exam-

[3] For a short epitome of the ideas of his main work in German see Posch 1923. Posch's main work appeared in the context of the intellectual war crisis. In a review of his book, published on the pages of *Nyugat* (Schöpflin 1915), it was emphasised that he was "the symbol of the rational character of scientists" in the context of the irrationality of the war. (It is symbolic that there is a picture of a wounded soldier on the neighbouring page of the book-review.)

ple of his anti-metaphysical ancestor, Karl Vogt, to suppose the existence of a pre-existent soul is similar to a hypothetic theory of the 'spirit of kidneys.' Urine is a product of kidneys, and we can offer an explanation of the production of it based on physiology of kidneys, without any supposed 'spirit of kidneys.' Thought is a product of human brains, and we can offer an explanation of the production of it based on physiology of brain, without any supposed 'spirit of brain,' (= soul, or mind). By Vogt's argumentation, both the 'spirit of kidneys,' and 'spirit of brain' (= soul, or mind) are useless hypotheses. By the opinions of Posch, Vogt's idea is not consequent, because of the usage of a separate entity called 'thought.' By him, we should use a new vocabulary, in which the word 'soul' can appear just as *cholera* in modern medicine. We know today that this illness is not caused by the black bile *(cholē),* and we use the word as a requisite of the school of Hippocrates. Similarly, we know that there is no entity called 'soul,' or 'psyche' as a cause of psychical phenomena, and we use the words 'psychology,' etc. just as requisites of old theories. Posch's thought is close to a today radical form of the theory of 'embodied mind,' or 'thinking bodies' (Lakoff and Johnson 1999); by him the word 'thought' refers just several actual or potential body-motions, without any qualitative differences from other motions. His theory, called *realism,* in his main work was focussed on the epistemology and anthropology, without a formulation of the moral consequences. Hungarian fictions of the war-trauma, influenced by him, and written in the circle of the above-mentioned periodical, is full of the questions of human identity, connected to the body-mind problem. They are stories about the *escape of the bodies from the prison of the soul (à la Foucault);* a falsification of the identity in our bodiless mind, only.[4]

An Application of Posch's thought to the Phenomenon of the Suicide

In the inauguration lecture he directly applies his philosophical anthropology for the special topic of suicide, with its consequences for the moral philosophy. The actuality of this topic in the Hungarian intellectual atmosphere of his epoch is clear by his initial words. Founder of the Hungarian Academy and its headquarters, where the lecture was read, died due to a 'successful' suicide.[5] By Posch, probably all the members of the audience – that is the Hungarian scientific élite – and the reader himself had a suicidal idea, at least once in their lives.

After this emotional introduction, Posch offers an overview of the classical opinions on the suicide from the history of the ethics (Stoics, Hume, Kant, Schopenhauer; and the Church Fathers, especially Augustine); then he refers to two important books on the suicide from the *fin de siècle*, that of Durkheim (1897), and of Masaryk (1881). (The last one had serious authority in Central

---

[4] For a typical example of this genre in a contemporary German translation see the novel of Frigyes Karinthy (Karinthy 1919).

[5] Count István Széchenyi (1791–1860).

Europe regarding this problem for several decades, not as a politician, but as a scientist.) A consequence of these new, sociological approaches for him was an evaluation of the phenomenon of suicide as a part of the negative side of the modernity, which needs a social solution. Posch agreed with these approaches, especially with Masaryk's diagnose which describes suicide as a societal phenomenon, as a consequence of the *half-educated cultural level of the large mass,* between the prohibition of suicide by the traditional morals, and a conscious, well-established resistance against suicide as the last remedy. Posch, based on the above-mentioned sources, observes that in the present (1921) state of the European civilisation, suicide is an ambivalent cultural phenomenon; on the one hand, by the common opinion, it is the last remedy of the human fate, and a horrible idea and scandalous moral act, on the other. However, by him, suicide is "an epidemic, which rages in the last centuries" (Posch 1921, 167); and he corrects Masaryk's old statistic data about small number of the Hungarian self-murderers (Posch 1921, 292); he does not discuss suicide from a sociological, empirical, but from a theoretical point of view. His lecture aim is to show an analysis of the false thinking of humans with suicidal ideas, and to offer a remedy against suicide by the demonstration of the logical absurdity of every possible suicidal idea.

By the chain of the ideas of his lecture, the deepest root of the suicidal ideas is a kind of the requisite of the faith of soul, or, by a pejorative expression, 'the faith of ghosts.' This culturally embedded requisite of the human thinking is the main obstacle of the complete understanding of the nature of our death, a transition from *persona* to *res*. The simplest case is the person who thinks about his death just as a radical amputation of the whole body from the soul; "who imagines that after his or her dead [...], he or she will levitate in the space [...], and for him or her the fact of suicide [...] will be the equivalent with the amputation of his or her legs in a critical case" (Posch 1921, 172). By his thought there are cases when the amputation of legs is better for other parts of the body; and there are cases when the amputation of the body is better for the remained part of the personality, called *soul*. By Posch, the recognition of the transition from *persona* to *res* is the only remedy for seeing the absurdity of these ideas. In his system there is no entity after death who could evaluate the qualities of the new circumstances, in comparison with the state of affairs before the suicide. All forms of the suicidal ideas calculate with this non-existing entity; a human with suicidal ideas always projects her or his present personality into an imagined future, after her or his successful suicide, and this projected pseudo-ego can enjoy the lack of the sufferings of the present, which is a better condition – in the imagination of the person who plans a suicide. By the opinions of Posch, understanding of the absurdity of this projection of our today *persona* to the tomorrow *res* of our cadavers is a better remedy against the suicidal thought than any traditional religious maxima of morals, based on the prohibition: "do not destroy, what was not created by you." By Posch, the 'faith of the soul,' which has been deeply penetrated in our culture, makes a double problem, concerning suicide. At first, it tempts the believers to make suicide with the hope of everlasting life, later this culturally embedded 'last remedy' must be prohibited by mere moral dogmas in the same culture. He recommends a more radical and consequent solution that is the rejection of the 'faith of the soul,' and basing the concept of a 'person' on his *realist philosophy*.

Epilogue: The Controversy of Milán Füst and Jenő Posch

Milán Füst in his reaction (Füst 1921) used the vocabulary of the "philosophies of life," and that of the "existential philosophy" transformed into a poetical essay. He requires free choice of individuals about their own death in extreme situations, and argues for the grounds of the subjective evaluation of the reality, saying that every world-view is a kind of *illusion,* without any privileged point of the objective observation. Füst's notes about the illogical nature of the reality precisely mark his horizon on the scene of the *fin de siècle* irrational philosophies.

Posch in his answer recovered the hidden philosophical roots of the thinking of his opponent: „the nowadays flourishing neo-Hegelianism [...] and its excellent representative, Bergson [...] replace the objective causes by sentimental emphases, [...] similarly to Milán Füst" (*On the Suicide;* Posch 1921a, 642). It is clear that by his opinion the irrational tendencies and subjectivity of the discussion paper puts his opponent into the group of the people who are 'faithful of ghosts.' These features of the point of view of Füst offer a possibility for projecting the person of the present into the cadaver of the future in the mind of a person with suicidal ideas.

Füst in his last article (*Afterword for the Question of the Suicide;* Füst 1921c) seems to recognise at least the requirement of an objective evaluation of the circumstances of the person who plans a suicide, but he does not give up the right for suicide in extreme cases. It is clear that they (Posch and Füst) think within the conceptual networks of incommensurable philosophical systems. By the "philosophies of life" of Füst, the supreme human right is a decision about the own life, including suicide, by the anthropology of the "realist philosophy" of Posch the free decision-making is an illusion under conditions when at the crucial point the required thinking person does not exist, and the cadaver in the same place cannot substitute this person.

It is interesting to see that their only common term is the *euthanasia*, based on ideas of a recognised German medical writer of their age, Hermann Nothnagel (1841–1905).[6] This word was typed by them always with Greek letters, as an

---

[6] A new edition of Nothnagel's widespread work on death was published in the year of the debate (Nothnagel, 1921). His lecture on the same topic has several Hungarian editions (Nothnagel 1905, 1914, 1915).

antique scholar philosophical expression for the "good death." In the following years of the twenties, after the death of Posch, the question of suicide seems to be dissolved in the problem of *euthanasia,* in the jurisprudential context. (For characteristic studies with references to Posch see the writings of Sándor Kéthelÿ: *Suicide and Euthanasia: Study of Criminal-Politics;* Kéthelÿ 1924; *Famous Suicides;* Kéthelÿ 1927.)*

References

Babits, M. 1918: A veszedelmes világnézet, *Pesti Napló,* 69/8, 1–4.
Durkheim, É. 1897: *Le suicide,* Paris: Félix Alcan.
Füst, M. 1921: Az öngyilkosságról, *Nyugat,* 14/6, 465–471.
Füst, M. 1921a: Az elmúlás kórusa, *Nyugat,* 14/7, 513–514.
Füst, M. 1921b: *Az elmúlás kórusa,* Budapest: Amicus.
Füst, M. 1921c: Utóhang az öngyilkosság kérdéséhez, *Nyugat,* 14/9, 724.
Karinthy, Fr. 1919: *Die Reise nach Faremido* [translated by St. J. Klein], Zürich: Rascher.
Kéthelÿ, S. 1924: *Az öngyilkosság és az euthanasia: Kriminalpolitikai tanulmány,* Pécs: Dunántúl.
Kéthelÿ, S. 1927: *Híres öngyilkosok,* Miskolc: Klen, Ludvis és Szelényi.
Masaryk, T. G. 1881: *Der Selbstmord als sociale Massenerscheinung der modernen Civilisation,* Wien: Carl Coregen.
McGuigan, Fr. J. 1978: *Cognitive Psychophysiology: Principles of Covert Behaviour,* Englewood Cliffs/NJ: Prentice Hall.
Nothnagel, H. 1905: *A halál* [translated by A. Schöpflin], Budapest: Lampel. 2nd ed.: 1915.
Nothnagel, H. 1914: *A halálról* [translated by B. Schmidt], Budapest: Kurcz–Fejér.
Nothnagel, H. 1921: *Das Sterben: ein Vortrag,* 4th ed. Wien: Perles.
Posch, J. 1896–1897: *Az idő elmélete,* Vol. I–II. Budapest: Dobrowsky–Franke.
Posch, J. 1915: *Lelki jelenségeink és természetük: Egy realista lélektan tervezete,* Vol. I–II. Budapest: Pfeifer.
Posch, J. 1921: Az öngyilkosság lélek- és erkölcstani szempontból, I–III. *Nyugat,* 14/3, 167–181; 14/4, 288–294; 14/5, 383–396.
Posch, J. 1921a: Az öngyilkosság ügyében, *Nyugat,* 14/8, 642–644.
Posch, Eu. [J.] 1923: Umriß einer realistischen Psychologie, *Archiv für die gesamte Psychologie,* 44/3 – 4, 191–243.
Schöpflin, A. 1915: Posch Jenő új könyve, *Nyugat,* 8/11, 625.

* This paper was supported by the Hungarian Scientific Research Fund (OTKA K 104643).

"… FOR SILENT AMONGST ROGUES, I SHARE THEIR VICE" – THE ROAD OF THE INTER-WAR HUNGARIAN JEWRY TO THE SHOA FROM THE ANTI-JEWISH LEGISLATION TO THE DEPORTATION

Gábor Kovács, *Budapest*

Historical-social context

Hungary, similarly to other Central-Eastern European countries in the 19th century, produced a lopsided social development. The old premodern social structures, the aristocracy, the gentry and the peasantry forming the overwhelming majority of the country, were coexisting with the new ones, the entrepreneurial and working classes. This coexistence involved special ethnical constellations; the capitalist class was recruited from non-Hungarian ethnical population; first of all it was the Hungarian Jewry which played the main role in economic modernization (Berendt, 1985: 32). As a result of the Jewish emancipation after the Austro-Hungarian Compromise (1867), the restricting premodern legal obstacles were removed from the way of the economic activity of the Hungarian Jewry which inhabited the socio-economic niches left empty by the Hungarian origin gentry possessing power positions of the state and public administration. There was a mutual interest-relation promising mutual benefits (Braham, 1985: 179): the traditional Hungarian elites needed an entrepreneurial class possessing the skills necessary for the smooth run of modern capitalist economy while the Jewry needed integration into Hungarian society which of course meant much more than mere possibility of unrestricted economic activity; it had social, cultural and emotional dimensions. All in all, these decades proved a Golden era in the history of the Hungarian Jewry (Braham, 1985: 178); but on the edge of the horizons were looming dark shades foreshadowing a much darker future.

The political strategy of state-induced assimilation, in reality, proved successfully only in the case of one ethnical group: it was the Jewry, the majority of which adopted the Hungarian identity in linguistic as well as in cultural meaning. (The ideology of *Magyarization* in other cases kicked back; it fuelled the national awakening of other ethnic groups and it involved growing political tensions.) Victor Karády, a Hungarian sociologist, an expert on the history of the Hungarian Jewry writes about a tacit assimilationist social contract:

"The 'assimilationist contract' demanded, in return, for integration and protection, a measure of "nationalization" on the side of the Jews, including their support for major national goals set by the ruling elite. Linguistic Magyarization, and the acceptance of an unbalanced political partnership, i. e., an arrangement under which the Jewish bourgeoisie could not reach political leverage in line with its economic strength. Most of the stipulations of this unwritten 'social contract' expressed both a relationship of reciprocal interests between Jewish and gentry elites and a measure of compulsion or constraint imposed upon Jews. It maintained not only the unchallengeable nature of the nobility's political hegemony but a subtly dosed – though in time somewhat diminishing – degree of exclusion of Jews from publicly controlled economic markets and civil service careers" (Karády, 1997: 148–149).

The former antebellum political strategy of liberalism based assimilation was replaced by ethno-protective politics in the interwar Hungary. It was rooted in the concept of national essence (Trencsényi, 2012: 70-120); they supposed an original national character which could be deformed or diluted by outer foreign influences; assimilation was deemed the most pernicious one of them. The war defeat, the disintegration of Historic Greater Hungary and the 'Jewish question' linked together in a fatal way in the contemporary Hungarian public opinion, fostered by the opinion of the leader intellectuals and political decision makers as well. If we are inquiring into the causes of emerging of such distorted intellectual-cultural-political climate, besides the political hysteria generated by the above-mentioned shock of the Trianon Peace Treaty (Kovacs, 2012), we have to mention the status anxiety of the so called Christian-national middle classes felt toward the Jewish-origin middle classes in the post-bellum shrank job market. (Karády, 1997) However, having accepted the logic of scapegoating seemed to be ineluctable the necessity of a segregative-discriminative anti-Jewish legislation.

The prelude was the *Law of Numerus Clausus* (1920) which restricted the proportion of the Jewish-origin students to 5 % in the higher education. The anti-Jewish legislation took place in three steps and every one of them was a new development in the way of segregation and isolation. The first ant-Jewish law was enacted in 1938; it defined the legal category of Jew on denominational basis and reduced the proportions of the Jews to 20 % in the business, trade and the professions, the second prescribed much lower proportions; the limit was drawn in 6 %, while the third one used racial terms. A decree issued on March 31st of 1944 obliged the Jewish persons to wear a yellow Star of David. The ghettoization and the deportation of the Hungarian Jews took place after the German occupation of Hungary on March 19th, 1944. Regent Horthy didn't resign and appointed a puppet government sustaining the pretence of legitimacy and legality. The deportation of the Hungarian Jewry of the countryside had been accomplished under German control, but by the direct participation of the Hungarian authorities; it was the Hungarian gendarmerie which played a main role in it. In the Nazi extermination camps, at last, about half a million Hungarian Jews died. The Jewry of Budapest escaped at the last minute in virtue of Regent Miklós Horthy who stopped the deportation.

This is a short historiography of the antecedents; it was the way leading to the Hungarian Holocaust, or Shoa, said in a nutshell. It is a description which is not able to give an explication of this tragedy. What happened? Who should share the responsibility for it? These questions need an approach beyond the level of the horrible facts. István Bibó, a Hungarian political thinker, one of the forefathers of Hungarian sociology tried to find answers in his long essay entitled *Jewish Question in Hungary after 1944*. It was published in 1948. Bibó suggested an overall national self-examination which really began, mainly in the circles of the Protestant churches. A debate took place in the contemporary press but it suffered an abrupt end after the communist takeover in 1949.

The interpretation of István Bibó

The way to Hungarian Holocaust was interpreted by Bibó in the referential framework of communal-political hysteria rooted in the shock of the dismemberment of the Historic Greater Hungary. His explicative model is a sociopsychological one moving on the level of inter-group relations and starting from the experiences got by the members of different communities from each other in social intercourse. (Bibó 1991) In this model the point of departure is the coexistence of a minority group of Jewish origin persons with a majority group of Gentile persons. These groups are constituted by the opposition of *We-consciousness* and *They-consciousness*. It is important that the assuming of we-consciousness for the members of minority group is, in many cases, not on a voluntary basis but it is ascribed to persons of special ethnic origins, peculiar behavioural patterns, profession, etc. by the members of the majority group. The genesis of anti-Semitism, in Bibó's model is due to the cooperative effect of three factors. The first of them is *prejudice* which, in Europe, had its origin in the medieval Christian antijudaism (The Jews as God-killers), the second one is the emerging of *distorted dehumanized social organization of society*; it is the situation which is labelled as a historical deadlock in Bibó's theory. These two factors in themselves are abstract; they concretize in the process of social intercourse when concrete persons encounter each other in concrete situations getting experiences about each other. *Experience* is, in Bibó's model, the third and, in a sense, the most important factor because it actualizes and enlivens the potentialities which are hidden in prejudice and distorted social organization of society.

Experience-gaining is a mutual process in the intercourse of inter-group contacts. The interpretation of experiences concerning out-group persons' behaviour patterns is accomplished by the referential codes of in-group rules, stereotypes and prejudices. This doesn't cause necessarily social troubles and dysfunctions in case there is a commonly accepted value-system which is able to function as a referential meta-framework transmitting between the different group codes. The self-correcting nature of experience-gaining, in this case, prevails; the ensuing experiences, statistically and in the long run, overwrite the former bad ones supposing that there are no lasting distorted social situations getting into contact different groups in such a way that they inevitably acquire false and misleading experiences about each other.

Bibó's illuminating and very appropriate example illustrating the nature of inter-group conflicts in a distorted social environment is the parable of the relation between *a housewife* and *a domestic servant*. (Bibó, 1991: 212-213). It was a typical social relation in the interwar Hungary; it was accustomed that the families of middle classes had their domestic servants. It was, in Bibó's concept, a typical case of a social contact based on distorted social organization; it blended a *Gesellschaft*-like contractual relation with a *Gemeinschaft*-like one. The speciality of it was the mingling of the rules of the premodern social contact with the modern one; as the main consequence of it the worst features of both dominated that hybrid relation but without their own advantages. Both parties acquired negative, unfavourable experiences about each other. The domestic servant, in the housewife's experience, was unreliable, lazy and had an inclination for lying and stealing, while the housewife, in the domestic servant experience, was domineering, capricious, with a predisposition for causeless sadistic behaviour toward her subordinate. These mutually disadvantageous negative experiences were real ones and the grievances of both parties caused by each other were real grievances, but this, emphasizes Bibó, doesn't mean the equality of these grievances. As the Hungarian sociologist, György Csepeli, in his analysis given about Bibó's theory of the genesis of Anti-Semitism points out:

"Bibó, of course does not forget to add that the relationship between the housewife and the domestic servant is an asymmetric one. Whatever they know and feel about each other, both partners are the captives of the structure, and their experience of each other is equally misleading. On the other hand, their grievances are not of equal seriousness. When it comes to a historical accounting of justice, their similar palpability will not prevent us from considering the complaint lodged by the domestic servant as the more valid" (Csepeli: 2001, 8).

The characteristics of the housewife–domestic servant relationship, mutatis mutandis, can be found in the Gentile–Jew relationship as well. As a consequence of the distorted social organization both parties offer their negative qualities for each other. The experiences acquired about each other, moreover, are interpreted by different interpretative codes between which there is no possible mediation or passage. The Jews, in sociological meaning, are among the causes of Anti-Semitism; their special, segregated social existence gives possibility for gaining false, misleading experiences for a wider society imbued with historic-origin anti-Judaism and burdened with the situations of a modern distorted social organization. The self-correcting nature of the process of experience-gaining in the case of Anti-Semites doesn't function properly. Experience, in this case, enlivens the abstract, inherited prejudice. The result is a fixation; it cannot be dispelled by the ensuing experiences. Every later encounter with Jews will be interpreted in the light of this fixation. However, it is important to add that, in Bibó's theory, the anti-Semite is not who doesn't like Jews. To be anti-Semite, for him, means to ascribe plots and conspiracies to Jews, to be convinced that they try to dominate the world, and to demand special measures against them.

When Bibó asserts that the behavioural patterns predetermined by a distorted social organization has been petrified into constant typical collective traits, his theory runs parallel with Hannah Arendt's concept about typical Jewish social roles emerging in the minority Jewish society embedding in the majority Gentile society (Arendt, 1958; Arendt, 1997). Both authors focus upon the problem of the relations of the Jewish communities with their wider environment and they share the same hypothesis: distorted inter-communal relations involve distorted communicative situations and false experiences concerning the other party. What is perceived by the social environment as greedy money making or hypercritical attitude, are traits emerging as responses of Jewish communities having been forced to marginal existence in premodern Europe, Bibó argues. Arendt, writing about the dichotomous Jewish types of *parvenu* and *pariah*, ascribes their emergence to the pressure of a wider social environment inducing typical behavioural patterns which can serve as survival strategies in a more or less hostile society.

Conclusion

Value-free sociological analysis and moral approach run together in Bibó's writing. The latter emerges on the basis of a sociopsychological model of intergroup relations in the interwar Hungarian society. The scientific method, for Bibó, is an intellectual tool helping him to pose the moral question of responsibility. His train of thought, according to this problem, runs on two levels. He insists, on the one hand, that responsibility can be assumed only personally by individuals; it makes no sense to allocate responsibility for wicked deeds committed by individuals to the whole community. The ideas of collective guilty and collective responsibility are not able to reach the goal of delivering usable criteria for a valid and well-founded moral judgement. When a nation is collectively declared guilty and it is collectively qualified responsible for wicked deeds the inevitable result will be the dispersion of guilty and responsibility. These moral categories can be used only for assessing individual acts performed by individuals. (Bibó's opinion is, in this respect, very similar to Hannah Arendt's one; after the World War II she also found out that it is meaningless to speak about collective German responsibility.) But the thing is not as simple as that. Bibó definitely calls for a national self-examination; it must be performed simultaneously with individual self-examination accomplished by the single members of the community. It is true that guilty and responsibility are the categories of individual morality, but the multitudinous moral failure of individuals in a critical situation indicates pathological, unhealthy state of the whole national community. This happened, Bibó asserts, in Hungary during the time of the persecution of the Hungarian Jewry. The most aching symptom was not the exceedingly great number of the direct perpetrators, but the exceedingly great number of the passive bystanders and onlookers who, either because of the hope for material and existential advantages or because of moral indifference, didn't help the persecuted Jews. Of course there were Hungarians saving and hiding the persecuted Jews and their number was not negligible, but general moral climate of the contemporary Hungarian society didn't foster and encourage such a kind of brave behaviour. Bibó raised the question of responsibility concerning the representatives of such vital social institutions as the public service and the Churches which, in his opinion, all in all displayed an insufficient and ambiguous behaviour. A great deal of intellectual elite of the interwar decades shared the traditional middle class origin cultural anti-Semitism and was not able to recognize in time the fatal consequences of the new type of racial anti-Semitism. (Ozsváth, 1997) All signs point to the direction that there was no generally accepted moral value system giving sure guidelines and moral supports in crisis-situation. However, the basic moral message of Bibó's writing is simple. It is the same as expressed by Mihály Babits, a great Hungarian poet, who before the war in 1938 - seeing that the country was running toward a catastrophe - in his monumental poem wrote about Jonah who was reluctant to accept God's calling, and put into the prophet's mouth the basic moral maxim:

> "for silent amongst rogues, I share their vice.
> Kin will be responsible for kin;
> Each man must go the way Thou sendest him."
> (Translated by István Tótfalusi)[*]

References

Arendt, H. 1958. *The Origins of Totalitarianism*, Cleveland: Meridian Books.

Arendt, H. 1997. *Rahel Varnhagen: the life of a Jewess*, translated by Richard and Clara Winston, Baltimore: Johns Hopkins University Press.

Berendt T. I. 1985. The Road Toward the Holocaust: The Ideological and Political Background. In: Randolph L. Braham and Bela Vago (eds.): T*he Holocaust in Hungary Forty Years Later*, New York : Social Science Monographs, pp. 31–42.

Bibó I. 1991. The Jewish Question in Hungary After 1944. In: Károly Nagy (ed.) *Democracy, revolution, self-determination:* selected writings/István Bibó, translation by András Boros-Kazai, Boulder, Co.: Social Science Monographs.

Braham L. B., 1985. The Uniqueness of The Holocaust in Hungary. In: Randolph L. Braham and Bela Vago (eds.): *The Holocaust in Hungary. Forty Years Later*, New York: Social Science Monographs, pp. 177–190.

[*] This paper was supported by the Hungarian Scientific Research Fund (OTKA K104643).

Csepeli, Gy. 2001. *Theory of Anti-Semitism Conceived by István Bibó*, http://www.csepeli.hu/pub/2001/csepeli_bibo_2001.pdf

Karády V. 1997. Identity Strategies Under Duress Before and After the Holocaust. In: Randolph L. Braham and Attila Pók (eds.), *The Holocaust in Hungary. Fifty Years Later,* [New York]: Rosenthal Institute for Holocaust Studies, Budapest : Institute of History of the Hungarian Academy of Sciences, pp. 147–178.

Kovacs G. 2012. Recollection, Forgetting, Reconciliation – The Hungarian Case. In: Janez Juhant & Bojan Zalec (eds.): *Reconciliation. The Way of Healing and Growth.* Wien-Zürich-Berlin: LIT Verlag, pp. 213–219.

Ozsváth, Zs. 1997. Can Words Kill? Anti-Semitic Texts and Their Impact on the Hungarian Jewish Catastrophe, in: Randolph L. Braham and Attila Pók (eds.), *The Holocaust in Hungary. Fifty Years Later,* [New York]: Rosenthal Institute for Holocaust Studies, Budapest : Institute of History of the Hungarian Academy of Sciences, pp 79–116.

Trencsényi, B. 2012. *The Politics of “National Character”: a study in interwar East European thought*, Milton Park, Abingdon; New York: Routledge.

IS DESTRUCTION OF A POLITICAL GROUP GENOCIDE? MASS KILLINGS IN SLOVENIA IN 1945

Tamara Griesser-Pečar, *Ljubljana*

"Genocide" is under international law classified as a crime since December 9th, 1948, when the Convention on the Prevention and Punishment of the Crime of Genocide was passed by United Nations. By definition then agreed on, genocide was classified as a crime committed in time of war or peace "*with intent to destroy, in whole or in part, a national, ethnical, racial or religious group*". (Art.2) This definition does not include the destruction of political and social groups, which is a sort of anomalism in international criminal law. They were not included because of the opposition of the communist countries, especially the Soviet Union. The Soviet Union wanted to prevent by all means any discussion about the victims of Soviet terror against the aristocracy, bourgeoisie, intelligentsia, Church, Cossacks, kulaks, Polish officers at Katyn etc. Millions of people – the estimated number varies, according to Stéphane Courtois about six million – died in Ukraine and adjacent Cossack territories in 1932 and 1933 because of starvation. The famine was not caused by bad economic policy or natural catastrophes, but because Stalin wanted to exterminate the social class of farmers, called kulaks. We speak here of "*extermination by hunger*" or Hodomor or even of "*famine-genocide in Ukraine*". Courtois sees great similarity between "*racial genocide*" and "*class genocide*". The death of an Ukrainian child, caused by Stalin's regime, so Courtois, weighs just as much as the death of a Jewish child in Warsaw Ghetto that died of starvation too (Courtois, 1997, 10). And in Slovenia we can add that a child that died of starvation in Sterntal or at Ormož Castle (Friedau) in 1945 is worth just as much as any other child that was a victim of such a crime. 39 children at the ages of four months to 12 years died in August and September 1945 at Ormož Castle – 17 of them were born in 1944 and 1945. (Leljak, 2012; Kozmos, 26.9.2013: 45) According to the project of Institute for Contemporary History in Slovenia "Death toll in the population on the territory of the Republic Slovenia during World War II and immediately afterwards" 47 children younger than seven were killed by the revolutionary side till the end of January 1946. (Deželak Barič, 2012)

But since the Convention on Genocide could not be passed without the Soviet Union, the United States gave in and the contested passage about political and social groups was dropped. Nevertheless we must put the question, whether the fact that international law has not yet included the political and social groups into the definition of genocide, automatically means that deliberate and systematic extermination of people with similar ideas and backgrounds is less condemnable as deliberate elimination of national, ethnical, racial or religious groups.

Many countries extended the definition of genocide in their domestic law to political and social groups also. In Slovenia the penal code states:

1. "Whoever, with the intention of destroying, in whole or in part, a national, ethnic, racial or religious group, gives orders to kill members of the group or inflict severe injury upon them, to cause serious bodily or mental harm to members of the group, to forcibly displace the population, to inflict upon the group conditions of life calculated to bring about its physical destruction in whole or in part, to impose measures to prevent births within the group, or to forcibly transfer children of the group to another group, or whoever, with the same intention, commits any of the above acts, shall be sentenced to imprisonment for not less than 10 to 20 years.
2. The same punishment shall be imposed on whoever commits any of the acts under the previous paragraph against a social or political group." (Uradni list RS, Nr. 50/2012)

Since its independence about 600 hidden graves have been found on Slovenian territory, but still not all have been discovered. The society and most of the governments till now showed little or no interest to find the responsible for crimes, dig the dead, give them a name and bury them in a descent manner. Of course because of that, noone was held responsible for the crimes.

World War II in Slovenia was rather complicated. We have to consider two levels. On one side the Slovenian territory was occupied by three powers – Germany, Italy and Hungary – and there was resistance of suppressed against the occupiers, but also, this overlapping, there was a second level, that is a fight between the suppressed about the right goal, about the right way of liberation, about the state- and social system under which the Slovenes should live after the war. In other words, in Slovenia there was the occupation and resistance, as well as revolution and counterrevolution. And the two levels cannot be separated. The Communist party, in numbers rather week but experienced in underground work – it was an illegal party in Yugoslavia since 1920 – saw in the occupation the only chance to gain power. The result was a bloody civil war. After the end of the war the communists came to power, but they continued what they had begun in 1941, that is, to eliminate everyone who would be able to take over the power after the war and question the aspirations of Communist party. At least 97.974 people lost their lives on the territory of the Republic Slovenia from the beginning of World War II until the end of January 1946. From May 1945 till the end of January 1946 15.089 Slovenes were victims of revolutionary terror, 13.842 of them were murdered immediately, others died because of the post-war treatment of repressive system, which is 15 % of all victims from 1941 on. (Deželak Barič, 2013: 69-80) To this number we have to add at least another 100.000 people of other Yugoslav nationalities who were killed after WW II and lie in one of the hidden graves. More than 10.000 victims, refugees – Home

Guards, Chetniks and civilians – in Carinthia who were handed over to the Tito troops were brought to communist concentration camps Šentvid and Teharje and most of them were executed without a trial and thrown into numerous hidden graves. (Mikola, 2013: 371)

Several historians, lawyers and political scientists again and again claim that the legal basis for the handing over of the Yugoslav refugees in Carinthia has to be sought in the war conferences of the Allies in Yalta and Potsdam. But this is absolutely not true, because the Big Three in Yalta – Winston Churchill, Stalin and Franklin Delano Roosevelt – did not negotiate about the repatriation of Yugoslavian refugees, they only spoke about putting into operation the Tito-Šubašić agreement signed on the island of Vis on June 16, 1944. The bilateral repatriation agreements signed in Yalta between Soviets and British and Soviets and Americans – later on also with French and Belgians – did definitely not refer to Yugoslavia. And the Potsdam agreement treated merely the repatriation of the Germans from Poland, Czechoslovakia and Hungary, not those from Yugoslavia. (http://www.documentarchiv.de/in/1945/potsdamer-abkommen.html)

The British handed over the Yugoslav refugees in Carinthia to the Yugoslav army without informing them about the rights they had according to the 1929 Geneva Convention and they made use of a deception, as they told the prisoners that they would be transferred to the British zone in Italy (Palmanova). They were well aware of their possible end. Young British captain Nigel Nicolson wrote in the log-book a day after their arrival in Viktring: "*None of them can be repatriated except to almost certain death at the hands of Tito.*" (Blumenwitz, 2005: 125-126) The civilians in Viktring were not returned by force, although the British in Carinthia planned to do so, but field marshal Alexander prevented that after his visit there practically in the last minute. Some civilians accompanied the Home Guards and shared their fate.

As Dieter Blumenwitz, expert on international law, pointed out in his expertise about Slovenia, that in 1945 the international law did not include a general prohibition of extradition of refugees. But that doesn't mean that countries could proceed arbitrary, they still had to respect the general human rights. Minimum standards according to Geneva Convention of 1929 and international law existed. There was also the Martens Clause as a part of the preamble to the 1899 Hague Convention. And according to this clause "*until a more complete code of the laws of war is issued [...]populations and belligerents remain under the protection and empire of the principles of international law, as they result from the usages established between civilized nations, from the laws of humanity and the requirements of the public conscience.*" (www.icrc.org/eng/resources/documents/.../57jnhy.ht)

However the handovers are classified, it can be agreed on, that not only the Yugoslav communists but also the British violated "*laws of humanity and the requirements of the public conscience*", although they are not now, sixty-eighth years later, prepared to admit their part in this tragedy. To repatriate war-prisoners or civilians against their will was an act of inhumanity.

Who were the people communists murdered during and after the war? They were anti-communists, adherents of the Catholic Church, among them also clergymen, members of the traditional pre-war political parties… Many saved their lives because they fled to Austria and Italy. Many of these refugees that settled down in Argentina, United States, Canada, Australia and in several countries in Europe, especially in Germany and Austria, were members of the pre-war traditional parties or their sympathizers or/and belonged to intelligentsia. In other words they were members of political and social groups.

Another problem that we have to consider under the aspect of genocide is the treatment of national minorities, explicitly the expulsion of their members. Great Britain was not the only country that send war-prisoners, refugees or so called "displaced persons", as they stated, "back home" after WW II. Discussion about this subject is still not possible in all involved countries. It is a great problem for example in the Czech Republic. As Blumenwitz pointed out: "*The moving of groups of people between the victorious powers was a common practice and led to new sorrows and unchecked acts of revenge after the end of the clashes.*" (Blumenwitz, 2005: 125-126) Although the Hague Convention did not regulate the deportations, it forbade, so Blumenwitz, "*considerably lower interventions in the liberty and honor*". He comes therefore to the conclusion, that "*deportations are quite inadmissible.*"(Blumenwitz, 2005: 65)

In the case of Slovenia/Yugoslavia we have to consider the expelling of Germans and Hungarian minority. Those who came to Slovenia as occupiers of course and were not Yugoslav citizens, had to leave the country after WW II, but there was no plausible reason or justification to expel members of the German or Hungarian minority, who had been Yugoslav citizens before the war, whose ancestors had lived there for any years, or even for centuries. This reminds of the way the Nazi-regime dealt with people. If certain German or Hungarian persons committed crimes, the courts were there to decide, but expatriation is something that should be condemned wherever it occurs. Not all Germans in Yugoslavia were Nazis, guilt is something subjective, objective guilt does not exist. The Article 2 of Genocide Convention is quite explicit. It includes members of a national or ethnical group and lists five categories:

> "(a) Killing members of the group;
>
> (b) Causing serious bodily or mental harm to members of the group;
>
> (c) Deliberately inflicting on the group conditions of life calculated to bring about its physical destruction in whole or in part;
>
> (d) Imposing measures intended to prevent births within the group;
>
> (e) Forcibly transferring children of the group to another group."

The arresting of Germans began in May and went on all June and July. Some were sent to prisons, but most were put into concentration camps. The most important concentration camp for Germans was Sternthal. From May till October 1945 there were about 10.000 internees – men, women and children, even babies and many old people –, most of them were of German nationality. Many were killed at arrival or later on, many died because of the bad conditions there: hunger, vermin, terrible hygienic conditions, infectious diseases like dysentery, diarrhea, typhus. (Leljak, 2012: 39) Several hundreds of Germans and some Slovenians were sent to concentration camps in Croatia and even Vojvodina. (AS 1931: šk.1062; Mikola, 2009: 10-16)

Acccording to Udba-report written in 1951, 9.474 Germans, Austrians and those of German origin, the so-called "Volksdeutsche" were deported in 1945 and 1946, among them also some Slovenes who were accused of collaboration with the occupiers. The author of this report, major Zvone Debevec acknowledged that "*mistakes*", as he called them, had been made, as such he mentioned the deportation of whole families regardless of the age because of a deed of one family-member. He also admitted that some were deported on the basis of unproven accusations. (Mikola, 2009: 10, 13) Roman Leljak, who was a member of the counterespionage troop and has done a lot of research work in the recent years, estimates that the number of deported persons was as high as 16.100. (Leljak, 2012: 33) Altogether 38.000 persons of German origin were deported, left Slovenia voluntarily or fled from the territory of Slovenia till the end of 1946. These includes also 7.000 Slovenes related to Germans or coming from mixed marriages and 9.800 Gottschee-Germans, who had been in 1941/1942 deported according to an agreement between Italy and Germany to the "Ranner Dreieck" or Brežice Triangle, that is the region known as the Lower Sava Valley in Lower Styria, because Gottschee lied in the Italian occupation zone. The Slovene inhabitants of the Brežice Triangle had been deported to Croatia, Serbia or Germany in 1941. (Leljak, 2012: 36-44) Germans in Brežice Triangle were also the first to be deported to Austria after the war, in the time between May and September 1945. The second wave of expulsions began in September 1945 and ended in October 1945. After the general elections in Yugoslavia on November 11 1945 the expulsions started again and the last Germans were transported over the border in November 1946.

Members of the Hungarian minority that lived in the region across the river Mura, called "Prekmurje" were also expelled from their homes – not from everywhere, the expulsions took place in District of Lendava. But there was a difference between the German and Hungarian minority. Members of the Hungarian minority were not forced to leave the country. The so called people's government transported the Hungarian minority members into concentration camps. First Hungarians were arrested already in April and put into concentration camp Filovci, the rest was arrested in July and came into several camps, 225 families landed in Sternthal. Altogether 558 Hungarians were expelled, among them 185 children younger than 15. In these concentration camps they experienced the same bad treatment as the Germans. But unlike them, they were allowed to return home in October 1945. (Mikola, 2009: 16-17)

References

Primary sources

Arhiv Republike Slovenije (ARS), AS 1931, Republiški sekretariat za notranje zadeve Socialistične Republike Slovenije, škatla 1062, Poročilo o selitvah volksdeutscherjev iz LRS v letih 1945-1946.

Uradni list RS, št. 50/2012 z dne 29. 6. 2012: 100. člen KZ-1-UPB2
http: //www.icrc.org/eng/resources/documents/.../57jnhy.ht..., 13.10.2013.

http://www.hrweb.org/legal/genocide.html, 22.09.2013.

http://www.icrc.org/eng/resources/documents/.../57jnhy.ht..., 13.10.2013.

http://www.documentarchiv.de/in/1945/potsdamer-abkommen.html, 13.10.2013

Literature

Blumenwitz, D. 2005, Okkupation and Revolution in Slowenien (1941-1946). *Eine völkerrechtliche Untersuchung, Studien zu Politik und Verwaltung,* Bd. 81, Wien-Köln-Graz: Bohlau Verlag.

Courtois S. 26.11.1997, "Hundert Millionen Tote", Frankfurt am Main: FAZ, p. 10.

Deželak Barič, V. 2012, "Consequences of Repression: Fatalities during World War II and Deaths Cause by it in Slovenia", paper read on the conference "*Repression during World War II and in the post-war period in Slovenia and in the neighbouring countries*" in Ljubljana on November 11, 2012.

Deželak Barič, V. 2013, "Smrtne žrtve druge svetovne vojne na Slovenskem in notranji obračun", *Odstiranje zamolčanega*, ed. Hančič, D.; Jenuš, G.; Strajnar, N., Ljubljana: Študijski center za narodnpo spravo 2013, 69–84.

Griesser-Pečar, T. 2013, "Der Vertrag von Jalta und die Auslieferung der Flüchtlinge im Mai 1945" [The Agreement of Yalta and the Handowers of the Refugees in May 1945], Ljubljana: Dignitas, in print.

Kozmos, K. 26th of Sept. 2013, "Komunizem: ideologija, ki je terjala otroška življenja", *Demokracija*, Nr. 39.

Leljak, R. 2012, *Verjagt. Ethnische Säuberung in Slowenien: Die Vertreibung der Deutschen in den Jahren 1945/1946*, Radenci.

Mikola M. 2009, *Dokumenti in pričevanja o povojnih izgonih prebivalstva v Sloveniji,* Ljubljana: Študijski center za narodno spravo.

Mikola, M. 2013, *Rdeče nasilje. Represija v Sloveniji po letu 1945*, Celje: Mohorjeva družba.

Nersessian, D. L. 2010, Genocide *and Political Groups*, New York: Oxford University Press.

Nicolson, N. 1998, *Long Life*, New York: Putnam.

SUICIDE IN THE ENVIRONMENT OF CULTURAL INDUSTRY

Tomas Kačerauskas, *Vilnius*

Introduction

Suicide is the result of a conflict between an individual and his (her) environment. The question is how this conflict emerges: by promising too much or by wishing too much, speaking about the individual? Anyway, the conflict shows the obstacles for a creative communication while an individual has been formed in his (her) environment as a certain "spoilage" that does not belong to it, or the environment does not allow being changed by a creative individual.

The chapter "Whether cultural industry is prophylaxis of suicides?" deals with the cultural industry and the media as an environment that forms an individual and that is full of promises of happiness. The question arises whether this environment, in which an individual has been "produced", gives a possibility of suicide for him (her): in the case of a product we cannot speak about such revolt against the system as suicide that is voluntary retreatment from service to the system. Promises of happiness also must purportedly prevent suicide that means refusal of the entertainments and pleasures.

The chapter "Production of happiness, control of the creators and phenomenon of suicide" deals with suicides in the context of a creative society and its control. On the one hand, suicide is a subject that doesn't surrender to any control. On the other hand, creator is a subject who at least doesn't feel cast-off by society that he (she) wants to re-create, that is why there is no reason to kill himself (herself). Nevertheless we can speak about suicide as a kind of creator's self-expression (self-creation) or as reaction to the deficit of creation.

Whether cultural industry is prophylaxis of suicides?

Cultural industry has been related with commercialising of culture, mass-production and consuming of cultural products, culture for the market. The term of cultural industry was introduced by T. W. Adorno in the thirties of the last century. A little bit later, in 1949 the text "Cultural industry" appeared in the book "Dialectic of Enlightenment" written by two emigrants from Germany M. Horkheimer and T. W. Adorno, who presented Frankfurt school (influenced by Marxism, too). This book expresses authors' critical approach towards culture, towards certain cultural forms that have been called cultural industry. What is cultural industry? First of all, this concept refers to commercialising of culture, mass production and consuming of cultural products. Thereby they have spoken about economic market for cultural mass products that inevitably influence the very concept and development of culture. Beside this, it presupposes the development of the media that forms cultural industry and culture in general, too. Although in the post-war West the media family consisted only from such now traditional media as newspaper, radio, telegraph, cinematograph, phone, photography, they have developed very fast and not without social order. Herewith every new media like a new child caused a change not only in the media family as a whole but also in all social relations and cultural layers. Communication by influencing the seeing and self-perception of society and an individual within it has moved into space somewhere between the media that have pushed aside existing man (woman) with his (her) worries, hardships and fears. On the one hand, a man (woman) has been liberated purportedly from his (her) existential worry with the help of the media; on the other hand, after removing of this worry, it has been removed also human creation, the source of which is temporal being towards death. As it seems the media, contrarily, has influence as compensation of mortality, prophylaxis of suicide, and promise of eternity. Hence, the very culture finally has been removed as a consequence of understanding of culture as cultural industry (regarding, at least, "authentic culture" and sense of a piece of art missed by M. Horkheimer and T.W. Adorno). (1984, 35)

Cultural industry as serial production of culture is possible under the conditions of the media. Beside this, the culture has been produced by the media that, while being "the extensions of man" (McLuhan 1994), begin finally to form a very man (woman) as the subject of consuming. In this way production replaces creation.

This criticism of cultural industry emerged already in industrial society, although influenced by the media. Beside this, cultural industry presupposes also the development of technologies. Cultural industry by appealing to economic relations presupposes herewith commercializing of cultural products, i. e. mass distribution, mass consuming served by new (information) technologies, and the media losing touch with its customers and dictating the rules for the society. After amalgam of these different elements of human culture, cultural product turns to commodity for buying and selling and this all finally eliminates the very culture.

As mentioned, the technologies influence inevitably cultural creation in a broad sense and art creation in a narrow sense. This influence is twofold: on the one hand, we face new sorts of art; on the other hand, the technologies by dictating new ways of creation and communication unify art. We face not only cinema, the roots of which are in industrial society, but also media art, video art, performances, installations, collages that reflect dynamic society, which turns to creative product of the media by communicating with the help of the media. Culture becomes inevitably a part of mass communication. The very culture serves as media, it is a certain medium for mass communication, in the background of which lies political ideology that seeks to occupy (produce) individual thinking and seeing. It seems that all this liberates an individual from existential responsibility and possibility of suicide.

We all, including customers and consumers of advertising, have not as much "rating thinking" (Bourdieu 2011) as rating complex: we do not want and cannot be free from the attitudes forced by mediated cultural industry, we are like the prisoners chained to the cave, in the wall of which we see the world in *The Republic* of Plato. However, the prisoners chained in a cave cannot only move their heads, but they also cannot kill themselves: not because of the fact that it is impossible physically but first of all because of the fact that they do not see any way on the wall of the cave.

Other side of cultural industry is entertainment and leisure industries. We can speak about creative aspects of entertainments but critics of cultural industry mention treason of cultural mission after culture and its creators orient towards entertainments and leisure by promising elixir of happiness for a mass consumer. According to M. Horkheimer and T. W. Adorno, cultural industry has been nourished by promises of happiness (1984, 161): it suggests the irritants that we need more and more intensive consumption although in reality that produces more and more distance from happiness. As a result, the following question arises: do the entertainment and leisure distance also from suicide?

Production of happiness, control of the creators and phenomenon of suicide

The cultural industry presupposes certain control of the creators. There are different methods of control and management including "harder" and "softer". One of them is financial leverages: bigger salary, premiums, money stimulations or penalties. Others are administrative punishments: reprimands, warnings, victimizations. By serving the machine of welfare's production there are also stimulating (acknowledgement, premiums) and disciplinary (penalties, forced labour, imprisonment) means in the society. The question is whether and how much punishment of separated members doing them unhappy contributes to production of general happiness. One criterion of general happiness is the index of suicides (number of suicides for certain number of population). The paradox is as follows: the societies of high welfare have high index of suicides. In other words, more intensive production of happiness we face in certain society more unhappy its members are. This phenomenon could be explained in this way: any production (even of happiness) is inseparable from the control that expropriates bigger and bigger part of private life's region for social region. As it seems the less private life is region of a person the less he (she) gives up on unsatisfied expectations of individual happiness.

Nevertheless the totalitarian society with high level of individual control (by narrowing at most the right to personal happiness) has low index of suicides. It could be explained not as far by successfully created happiness (to be precise, mechanism of happiness' control and monitoring) as by individual resistance to this mechanism: the resistance is inseparable from objective to survive under any conditions and could be related with individual creative intensions in not creative (totalitarian) society. Here we face two ideas: 1) a "hard" control of individuals is alien to a creative society; 2) a creative society is not a society of happiness' production while it controls its producers strongly. Contrarily, an individual is happy as much as he (she) is free (but not forced) to contribute to creation (but not production) of happiness' environment. This freedom has been witnessed in paradoxical way by wish of the creators to choose death on their own[1]. On the other hand, the use of freedom to die could be related also with deficit of creation and with abruptness (including emotional ones) of creative activity.

Suicide in general is the revolt of an individual against attempt of the society to control him (her). Nevertheless one or another society treats even suicide as the subject of its control. From the point of view of economic society every employable being's suicide is a spoilage of happiness' production. From the point of view of knowledge society, suicide means a broken chain of knowledge transferring. From the point of view of mediated society, suicide is an extension of nothingness. From the point of view of entertainment society, suicide is a gamble from death. From the point of view of consumer society, suicide is a consumer of death. From the point of view of postmodern society, suicide is a victim of remnant industrial relations. Suicide for creative society is both, an author of extreme self-expression (self-creation) and a creator frustrated by creative deficit. However, creative society covers the aspects of other mentioned societies: it is also economic, knowledge, entertainment, consumer, postmodern society that balances on the edge of suicide, too. Creative society oriented towards creation is not safeguarded from its extremes that try to cover being and nothingness. To rephrase M. Heidegger[2], an authentic creation is a creation towards death. However, a creation towards death is a creation of life fullness instead of abort of the life. That is why the creation towards death is prevention of suicide having in mind being to be created. And contrarily, hectic search for death's alibi by changing economic, knowledge, media, entertainment, consuming trains forces finally to jump from the life train.

One of happiness' indicators is low index of suicide. If happiness was proportional to material welfare this index would be the less the richer is society. Unfortunately this is not the case. A good example is Lithuania that is not nearly the last one in the club of the richest countries (as could be held European Union)[3]. Nonetheless Lithuanian society is one of the unhappiest in the world be-

---

[1] Remember the death of E. Hemingway, S. Zweig, R. Gary and other creators.

[2] *Das eigentliche Seinkönnen* (Heidegger 2006, 267).

[3] In 2012, according to the gross domestic product for one person Lithuania is richer than Romania, Bulgaria, Croatia and other Baltic countries.

cause of the one of the highest index of suicides. My hypothesis is that this index could reflect the level of creativity in certain society, although in negative sense. Creativity is prevention of suicide: the creators by projecting their identity towards future pieces of art are distanced from the Self dissipated by the circumstances, that is why they are not lost in alien environment and they do not feel that they are unnecessary appendage of this environment. Contrarily, the creators are also the creators of their social house; they are convinced that the society doesn't exist without them. This idealism does not presuppose any arrogance of the creators: nobody is so self-critical as the persons who "know nothing" by doing art. Contrarily, it presupposes responsibility for environment to be created and the Self to be created within it.

Nevertheless the creators are always "left" their house (*oikos*) that should be cared by looking for the resources for them, i. e. ideas. The content of *oikos* as the house of the creator changes not because of social progress that has been related often with economic achievements and material welfare, in other words, with plenty of things while they have been multiplied by the media. The content of *oikos* changes because of creative alternation while the creators are looking for the ideas both in the past and the future. That is why a creator is homeless, i. e. beyond the economy, the hardships of which does not influence the creation in a negative way. Thereby the economic shortages do not increase risk of creator's suicide. Rather contrarily: during the economic and political crises emerge beautiful pieces of art. There are a lot of examples in the civilizations during the political decline. Another kind of example is prosperity of culture in interwar Europe during the economic crisis. However a creator being homeless (anti-economy) is also at home everywhere (beyond economy), if he (she) finds the creative ideas, i. e. the instruments, everywhere. Nevertheless that "everywhere" after world becomes global turns into "nowhere", in which every creation has been swilled. Rather that "everywhere" should be related with more or less local environment formatted by national or regional policy.

Creative policy should be cherished from both tactic and strategic reasons. The last ones should be related with the creation of a creative society, the first ones – with happy society without suicides. If creation has certain therapeutic function (reduction of sufferings), for instance in the sense of suicide prevention, it is already good enough reason to cherish and stimulate creativity. Actually, these tactical arguments are stronger than strategic ones, i.e. than the aim to form certain utopian creative community. Nevertheless utopia or *atopos* (no place) delivers for a creator the house "everywhere", at least in social environment to be reached in one pole by the members of creation.

Not all creators have bent for risk that could be related with suicides, too. Although physical and creative risks have the similitudes, between them are certain tensions and contradictions. The creator who appreciates his (her) activity avoids unnecessary physical risk that could collapse his (her) creation. We can speak here even about reverse proportionality: the more risk is the creation the more careful is his (her) author in physical sense. Even regarding the media, a creator understands that it unnecessary ventures for his (her) creation. That is why he (she) usually avoids publicity although it helps to promote his (her) creation. However, the media could distance from the creation, as mentioned when speaking about creative industry. The creators, who appreciate their creation, do not intrude in any venture that is risky from the point of view of suicides.

Beside this, intensive creation satisfies the need of venture and adventures, that is why the challenges of physical nature turn to unnecessary luxury instead of attractive amusement. The same could be said about such anti-sportive tests as alcohol and drugs. That is why the creator seems to be boring. He (she) is boring being sunken into his (her) creative dreams, i. e. is "left" from his (her) physical and social environment, while he (she) seems to be sullen. Creation nourishes him (her) even with too big doses of risk and venture – there is no more need to ask them from such dealers as the media and publicity. Sometimes there is threat of a creative overdose and convulsions of forced abstinence that lead to alcoholism, drug addiction and even suicide.

Recreation is an aspect of a responsible being: final leave of a hero after suicide does not give any possibility to change his (her) life environment, herewith – his (her) life within it. Eternal leave does not allow radical changing his (her) life herewith changing his (her) environment: suicides see conserved both themselves and their society and do not seek to recreate any of them.

Conclusions

It seems that an individual has no preconditions for suicide in the environment of cultural industry: he (she) is a product of this system that produces happiness. What is more, suicide has been treated as an asocial element that disturbs economic, communication, consuming, and entertainment relations. We can treat suicide also as extreme creativity by revolting against industrial (i. e. not enough creative) relations in the society of the production of happiness. Nevertheless suicide is rather an expression of creative deficit: suicide does not see any more possibility to recreate him (her) or the society. Society of the production of happiness has namely such deficit of creativity.

References

Baudrillard, J. 1983: *Les strategies fatales*, Paris: Grasset.

Baudrillard, J. 1976: *L'échange symbolique et la mort*, Paris: Gallimard.

Bourdieur, P. 2011: *Sur la télévision*, http://www.youtube.com/watch?v=vcc6AEpjdcY

Fiske, J. 1997: *Introduction to Communication Studies*, London and New York: Routledge.

Flusser, V. 2007: „Vorlesungen zur Kommunikologie", in *Kommunikologie*, Frankfurt am Main: Fischer Taschenbuch Verlag, pp. 233–351.

Heidegger, M. 1996: *Being and Time*, New York: State University of New York. Translated by J. Stambough.
Heidegger, M. 2006: *Sein und Zeit*, Tübingen: Max Niemeyer Verlag.
Horkheimer, M.; Adorno, T. W. 1984: „Dialektik der Aufklärung“ in Adorno, T. W. Gesammelte Schriften, Bd. 3. Frankfurt am Main: Suhrkamp.
McLuhan, M. 1994: *Understanding Media: The Extensions of Man,* Cambridge: The MIT Press.

THE INTERTWINE OF INTEGRATIVE AND NORMATIVE POTENTIAL OF RELIGIOUS ORGANIZATIONS IN CONSTRAINING SUICIDAL BEHAVIOUR

Rafal Smoczynski, *Warsaw*

Introduction

Emile Durkheim who started the scientific discussion on the function of suicide in social change, in his classic study "Le Suicide" ([1897] 1951) used suicide rate variable as an indicator of the disintegration of social ties (egoism) and deregulation of the normative structure (anomie). In fact, Durkheim in his analytical typology defined four types of suicidal acts: anomic, egoistic, altruistic and fatalist, out of which altruistic and fatalist are characteristic for pre-modern societies and anomic and egoistic occur in the modern societies mainly during socio-economic crisis, which decomposes normative and regulative framework of the society or when the integrative bound of social groups (kin, family, religion) significantly weakens - than the rate of egoistic suicides increases. Subsequent sociological scholarship rendered the analytical distinction between anomie (weakened social control) and egoism (weakened social integration) as problematic, namely, there is a number of authors who claim that these categories are closely related, particularly in empirical setting and their separation is not justified (e.g. Pope 1976, Johnson 1965). In this paper I also deem this separation of little importance.

Durkheim while analysing the crucial role of "social bound" in protecting community against anomie, offered an assessment of three major European denominations of his era in their integrative potential guarding against suicide, with Catholicism as an example of the most integrated group in comparison with Judaism and Protestantism. Although Durkheim assumed that different denominations represent unequal power in protecting their members against the risk of suicide, he did not seem to be substantially interested in normative aspects of Catholicism, Protestantism, or Judaism. His major concern was with integrative power of religious organizations, that is to say, he analyzed how religious organizations effectively ordered daily life of individuals embedded within the given religious community. Catholicism according to him did better job in terms of its integrative potential than Protestantism and Judaism and consequently he asserted that Catholics had lesser suicidal expectancy. This narrow integrative potential that stands in the centre of Durkheimian interest was neatly grasped by Breault (1986: 640): "Durkheim's concept of social integration refers to the magnitude and intensity of people's ties or connections to one another (shared values being an important element in this)... [T]he more that people associate in religious societies or denominations, the higher the social integration is. Group association or membership is accordingly the key to Durkheim's theory of social integration. Catholics, for Durkheim, are more integrated because Catholicism as a traditional religion permits greater connectedness among believers.

State of the Arts

Since seminal intervention of Durkheim numerous sociological studies have been conducted to test if religion has an independent effect in lowering suicide rate and the results of these explorations have been far from being conclusive. There is a wealth of literature, especially quantitative, arguing that religion alone does not act as an independent variable in reducing suicidal expectancy, Stark and Bainbridge (1982) suggested that suicide is positively correlated with urbanization and increased education, Simpson and Conklin (1989) in their review of the literature on religion and suicide concluded that the modernization is the key variable in understanding who commits suicide. A number of researchers debunked the crucial Durkheimian notion of superior efficiency of Catholicism in protecting against suicide: in fact little difference was found between Catholicism and Protestantism in their capacity of reducing suicidal tendencies (e.g. Pope, Danigelis 1981). On the other hand, contradictive findings were reported. Breault (1986) drawing on extensive data covering span of 47 years in the US found support for Durkheim's social integration thesis that Catholic church membership significantly reduces the risk of suicide, and these findings seem to be even more important when - as Breault notes - we take into account that Catholics committed less suicide than non-Catholics during the long period of time when society has been through rapid social change. Also in Pescosolido & Georgianna's (1989) article low suicide rates were reported for Catholics and Evangelical type of Protestants while Judaism and mainstream Protestantism did not exert consistent hindrance on the suicide risk.

Criticism

Ambiguous results of the above mentioned studies have raised criticism about their methodological appropriateness. Critics have noted that important variables in quantitative studies were ignored, also quality, reliability and comparability of data have been questioned (Breault 1986). A number of studies were not representative, very rarely samples were collected in the cross national context, mainly American and other advanced capitalist societies were studied. Pescosolido (1990) in turn noticed a bias that underpinned some studies undertaken within the implicit secularization perspective what produced simplistic analytical strategies framed according to the logic of negligible impact of religion upon the contemporary society. Secularization thesis as we know is profoundly spurious and in its orthodox form has been largely neglected in contemporary literature (Casanova 1994). Nowadays sociological approach as Pescosolido (1990: 339) notes demonstrates rather differentiated logic of religious agency operating in modern societies, which are marked by secularization but also by religious growth, revivalism and continuity. Keeping in mind that the monolithic indicator of church membership embracing large aggregate samples is far from being ideal in testing the integrative potential of religion constraining suicidal expectancy (Bertault 1986) and particularly while criticising the overwhelming secularist bias it seems that more promising approach to the interplay between religion and suicide has to bring into light a multi-dimensional aspects of religious practices and their possible potential of impacting suicidal tendency behaviour.

Firstly, keeping close to the recent developments in the existing research we have to acknowledge that religious integration variable should be conceptualized beyond the basic undifferentiated category of religious affiliation which usually in surveys implies self-declaration of religious identification. The more refined approach should rate rather the degree of religiosity and the extent of commitment to church-related activities. The simple declaration of religious identification – as Hong (1981) showed – does not provide any meaningful findings informing about the impact of religious organization on anomie, while frequency of religious attendance, that marks importance of networking among co-religionists brings significant results informing how specific type of religious commitment may reduce the degree of risk of anomic suicide. This more specific approach gives especially interesting results – as Stack and Kposowa (2011) demonstrated – for individuals who attend religious services several times a week where the suicidal expectancy is the lowest while for those who never attend score highest on the suicidal expectancy rank. The importance of frequency of attendance of religious services and the position of religious networks, that is the frequency of spending time with co-religionists as measures of religious commitment in affecting negatively pro-suicide attitude, was also supported by other authors (eg., Pescosolido 1990; Pescosolido and Georgiana 1989; Stack and Wasserman 1992).

Secondly, it is not enough to divide samples into different denominations, it is also necessary to grasp the sub-denominational differences which allow to properly conceptualize the integrative aspect of the religious organization in its potential of reducing suicidal risk (Hong 1981). For example, as recent literature shows, particularly Pescosolido and Georgianna (1989) and Pescosolido (1990), assuming a unified integrative potential of contemporary Protestantism is clearly empirically untenable, in fact contemporary Protestantism has considerably changed from the times when Durkheim asserted that Protestantism provides a weaker integrative basis compared with Catholicism, at least since the emergence of new revival protestant movements. These new groups as compared with liberal currents of Protestantism demonstrate a relatively strong normative and integrative potential, also in regard to its potential of reducing risk of suicide. What links these revivalist movements is the belief in the personal relationship between God and man, a relatively demanding moralism and the powerful experience of conversion that divides the sinful past and the present Christian life. This new movement called Great Awaking of Pentecostal Protestantism except for traditional emphasis put on the importance of Holly Scripture places also on the "gifts of holly spirit" (e.g. speaking in tongues, prophecy, healing, exorcism as a part of daily spiritual welfare with demons, baptism in Holly Spirit, fighting with the local "demonic cultures") (Robbins 2004).

Some authors (Pescosolido, Georgianna 1989: 34, 45) rightly indicate that also contemporary Catholicism itself has been considerably differentiated from the time when Durkheim took it as an ideal type of the religious group protecting from suicide. It is necessary to properly situate Catholicism which was of concern for Durkheim in the historical contexts of the late XIX century when the Church presented much more homogenous shape in terms of doctrine and discipline. Its coherency - that was appreciated by Durkheim - should be understood in the light of "the modernist crisis" against which Church was waging a battle. This militant attitude that attracted Durkheim's attention contributed to the increase of normative discipline and enhanced integrative potential among Catholics that was greater comparing with the internally differentiated shape of post-Vaticanum Secundum Catholicism which varies in many respects from the late XIX century Church. Any contemporary analysis involving aggregated samples of Catholicism should be thus treated with suspicion.

Normative aspect

Now the question remains about the normative teaching of religious organizations and weather it offers a suicide risk reduction potential the way normative aspect does. Let's consider the case of contemporary conservative Protestant communities. It has been tested on several occasions that they continue to be protective against suicide what apparently might be related to their conservative teaching which as - it was sometimes suggested – is more efficient in hindering anomie than liberal attitude of mainstream Protestant communities. Pescosolido and Georgianna (1989) answering this question argue that this is mainly the strength of religious network ties that should be perceived as a crucial agency influencing individuals' attitudes and eventually the integrative aspect of religious organization reduces anomie. Conservative Christians are more active in participating in religious life than mainstream Protestants who do not attend church services frequently and do not network with their co-religionists the way it is practiced among conservative Protestants and Catholics and "this participation in networks varies in ways consistent with the protective or aggravating effect of religions on suicide" (Pescosolido, Georgianna 1989: 43). Therefore, the impact of doctrinal teaching alone is not of utmost importance because - as they argue - conservative denominations do not condemn suicide more than liberal denominations: "What separates religious groups is the degree to which practices conform to original dogmatic prohibitions. This depends fundamentally on the nature of the religious community and on ties that bind individuals to it. Moral rules must be backed by a cohesive community to endure; without it, beliefs, loyalties, and identities erode" – explain Pescosolido and Georgianna (1989: 40).

But it would be wrong to assume that suicidal protection is uniquely related to integrative component of the religious group. This paper in line with the recent studies exceeding Durkheimian perspective of "social ties alone" argues that normative teaching of religious communities did matter indeed. To grasp an efficiency of normative aspect that protects against suicide it is important to look how integrative potential overlaps with the normative component and through this merger religious organization guides social action. Here comes as handy recent Lim and Putnam's (2010) findings providinig extensive data on the role of religious practices on shaping well being of the members of religious organizations. These findings on the one hand confirm classic Durkheimian argument that the religious organization shapes well being of individuals due to its social networking, but what is equally important, it reveals a unique function of the normative aspect of religious organization in improving well being of religionists. As Lim and Putnam argue it is impossible to explain religious organization's efficiency in improving quality of co-religionists' life that would be limited only to protecting effect of social ties' strength. They demonstrate that religious organizations offer different quality of social resources comparing with the secular social networks, and due to religious normative teaching provide a greater sense of comfort to co-religionists who use similar interpretative framework of reality: "People who frequently attend religious services are more satisfied with their lives not because they have more friends overall [...], but because they have more friends in their congregations" (2010: 920). Lim and Putnam (2010: 920) thus suggest that: "<sitting alone in the pew> does not enhance one's life satisfaction. Only when one forms social networks in a religious congregation it leads to a higher level of life satisfaction." Thus, what has been already revealed in Hong's study, that religious identity alone does not reduces the risk of suicide may found its follow up in Lim and Putnam's study (2010: 923) who demonstrated that "strong religious identity makes little difference on life satisfaction unless it is supported by a group of close friends in one's congregation". Only when two factors are in the same place it makes a difference: "When people have both a strong sense of religious identity and within-congregation networks does religion lead to greater life satisfaction" (2010: 923-924).

Conclusion

According to the growing amount of gathered data on the relationship between religion and suicide risk it seems that this is the mutual reinforcing effect of religious normative aspect and tangible networking that reduces suicide expectancy among religionists. We find a very compelling example of this synergy effect between strong religious identities and social networks in "communities of faith" provided by Lim and Putnam study. Being involved in these communities enhances the well being of churchgoers and through this it may also protect from suicide since people enjoying greater life satisfaction are less prone to commit suicide. It is relevant to conclude citing Lim and Putnam (2010: 927): "It is neither faith nor communities, per se, that are important, but communities of faith. For life satisfaction, praying together seems to be better than either bowling together or praying alone".*

References

Breault, Kevin 1986. Suicide in America: A Test of Durkheim's Theory of Religious and Family Integration, 1933-1980 in *American Journal of Sociology* 92(3): 628-656.

Casanova, Jose. 1994. *Public Religions in the Modern World.* Chicago: Chicago University Press

Durkhim, Emile. [1897] 1951. *Suicide.* New York: Free Press

Hong, Lawrence. 1981. "Anomia and Religiosity: Some Evidence for Reconceptualization" in *Review of Religious Research*, 22(3): 233-244.

Johnson, Barclay. 1965. "Durkheim's One Cause of Suicide" in *American Sociological Review* 30:875-86.

Lim, Chaeyoon, Putnam, Robert D. 2010. "Religion, Social Networks, and Life Satisfaction" in *American Sociological Review* 75(6): 914-933.

Pescosolido, Bernice, Georgianna, Sharon. 1989. "Durkheim, suicide, and religion: Toward a network theory of suicide" in *American Sociological Review*, 54(1), 33-48.

Pope, Whitney, Danigelis, Nick. 1981. "Sociology's 'One Law'" in *Social Forces* 60: 495-516

Pope, Whitney. 1976. *Suicide: A Classic Analyzed.* Chicago: University of Chicago Press.

Robbins, Joel. 2004. "The Globalization of Pentecostal and Charismatic Christianity" in *Annual Review of Anthropology* 33: 117-143.

Simpson, Miles, Conklin, George. 1989. "Socioeconomic Development, Suicide and Religion: A Test of Durkheim's Theory of Religionand Suicide" in *Social Forces* 67(4): 945-964.

Stack, Steven, Wasserman, Ira. 1992. "The effect of religion on suicide ideology: An analysis of the networks perspective" in *Journal for the Scientific Study of Religion* 31(4):457–66.

Stack, Steven, Kposowa, Augustine. 2011. Religion and Suicide Acceptability: A Cross-National Analysis in *Journal for the Scientific Study of Religion* 50(2): 289–306.

Stark, Rodney, Bainbridge, William S. 1982. "Toward a Theory of Religious Commitment" in *Journal for the Scientific Study of Religion* 19:114-2.

Stark, Rodney, Daniel P. Doyle, Jesse Lynn Rushing. 1983. "Beyond Durkheim: Religion and Suicide" in *Journal for the Scientific Study of Religion* 22: 120-131.

* It is acknowledged that this paper is a part of the Polish National Science Centre's funded project NN116695440 "The impact of Catholicism on attitudes and economic action of Polish entrepreneurs", project nr. 6954/B/H03/2011/40.

SUICIDE OF EUROPEAN CIVILIZATION

Mari Jože Osredkar, *Ljubljana*

Introduction

We will talk about the suicide of European civilization. Perhaps this claim seems exaggerated, but events in Europe show that man of the "old continent" that was once teeming with Christian faith and Christian life, abandoned religious practice and has maintain just Christian values which he calls human rights. This process is called secularization in society. We wonder why secularization occurs. Compared with the Islamic society where secularism does not come up to such an extent as in Europe, we make the hypothesis that the cause of secularization is hidden in the interpretation of God's revelation. God's Commandments are interpreted by the European society very freely and that is leading Europe to liberalism, which has escaped the foundation (God) for "human rights" that is for ethics, and has entered into the culture of death.

European and Slovenian actual situation

Some moralists and ethically conscious people pay particular attention to a few small things in the work of politicians who want to build the European Union. These things appear negligible to a superficial observer. But, in fact, we consider them very important for the future of Europe and our civilization. We can mention, for example, the adoption of the European Constitution. The problem began with the question: Should the words "God" or "Christianity" be mentioned in its text or not? The ardent discussion ended with the recognition that today Europeans do not have shared common values. A similar polemic was the so-called Berlin Declaration, formally adopted by the Heads of European States and their Governments on the 50th anniversary of the EU on 25th March 2007 in Berlin. On this occasion, the German Chancellor said on German television ZDF that the declaration did not mention the Christian God, because "we do not want to have a provocative statement, but we want to highlight just that which unites us." So they inserted in the declaration just a text that talks about climate change, the protection of borders and the common European currency, the Euro. While the U.S. president makes an oath of office on the Bible and on the dollar bill it is written "In God We Trust," Europe is hesitant to mention God in its documents.

It is the same in the Slovenian society. We witness not only in past history, but also today, cases and trends to make religion a private, hidden human activity. And it is not only religion as man's relationship with God, but also and especially the values of faith and religious expressions. If Christians in Slovenia, for example, raise their voice in the defence of unborn children, they are marked as partisans of totalitarian ideology that oppose the values of modern society. For example, on 15th March 2013, the Slovenian National Assembly held a public debate on "hate speech." Some persons drew attention to the hate speech that encourages violence against unborn children. The Chair of the Commission for Petitions, Human Rights and Equal Opportunities stopped them and accused them of espousing hate speech. In Slovenia and the European continent, we can surely speak of the emergence of secularism and secularization.

Secularism and Secularization

In Catholic culture, the word "secularization" designates the transition of consecrated persons to secular status. The Latin term "saecularis" means secular. From this signification evolved the word "saecularisatio." The expression started to be used somewhere between the 17th and 18th centuries, in connection with Church property which passed into the care of State. In this sense, today the secularization infers "the transformation of something religious to the secular state," even if we have "acquisition of Church property by the State" (Flere and Kerševan 1995, 122). In fact, by this expression we speak also of the "independence of activities, which in the past were under the control of the Church" (Sruk 1995, 296). In recent decades, the word secularization has been often used for defining the dechristianisation of Western European Christian society. A secularized society or person is one who has in the past publicly expressed religious values, but now forgoes overt religious teaching (Flere and Kerševan 1995, 123-124), but he may follow them just in his private life. This is then a society where religiosity and secular are separated. This is not anti-religious stance, or the suppression of religion, but the actual separation of the public life from religion, which is known as the principle of "separation of Church and state." This separation could ensure the autonomy of both institutions. The Church does not enter into political decisions, and the State is not concerned with the internal organization of the Church and its teachings. In this case, secularization does not mean the exclusion of the Church from society. But, it seems that the term secularization in Europe and in the Slovenian context tends to express something more than the separation between religiosity and secular life.

The process of separation between public and private life in the field of religion sooner or later leads to a situation where religious thinking and religious institutions become less relevant to society, marginalized, and even driven out of public life. There is no public talk about God and religion is not publicly expressed. The religiosity in society is replaced by rationality.

Till this moment, we have talked about the process which religion increasingly alienates from public life. Until this process is going on "spontaneously" it can be denoted by the term secularization. However, when this process becomes a movement or ideology we call it secularism. Secularization is founded upon political and philosophical situation in the 19th century. This was the time of increasing social tensions between working class and capitalist class, bigger and bigger restrictions of political and religious freedom, more and more intense dispute on the relationship between faith and reason etc. This situation gave birth to political secularism.

The concept of revelation as the key to understanding of secularization

There is a big difference between the Christian and Islamic conception of revelation. It helps us to understand why we have secularization in the Christian world and why there is no secularization in the Islamic world. If we compare the written revelation of the two religions, we find that the Bible had been created for many centuries earlier. In fact, the Jewish revelation had passed down from generation to generation through oral tradition. Also the written record of revelation was subjected to revisions. Considering that the Jewish canon of Tanakh was finally completed only in the second century after Christ, this means almost two thousand years of the formation and of the wording of divine revelation. Therefore, this is not a literal dictation of God's word, but rather the formulation and the gradual recognition of what God wants to communicate to humanity. In the Old Testament prophets preached the word of God. Also, Christianity knows the scriptural teachers who provided the apostolic proclamation. “Christians believe in God who has revealed himself through Jesus Christ, and we find out about Him after the testimony of the Apostles and the Church. Therefore, it is our faith that first pushes us to hear about God. But this listening is not direct, it is always mediated through people. God does not come to us or speak to us through unusual events, creatures, and objects, but quite simply through man. The mediator between man and God is another man who has already responded to become his divine messenger” (Ocvirk 1990, 135). The prophet is the “mouth of God” through which God speaks to man. The word of God is for all people. The prophet is only the first to discover and reveal what God wants to reveal to all (Torres 2010, 42). The Prophet therefore is a man of faith who recognizes God's will, whether through the word of man or a deed, and when convinced of its authenticity, he declares it to the people as the word of God. This is his mission. In order that his testimony of God's word will be authentic, the Prophet must be the first person to achieve dialogue with God and realize the word of God in his life. From this personal dialogue and from this connection to God his mission is defined. But the Prophet is not a simple interpreter who “translates” God's secrets to people. He is not a theologian who translates the mind of God into doctrine. Prophets are those who love God, and this love is transformed into a mission. The Prophet is chosen and he must take his mission as the essence of his life. Martin Buber stresses the “enthusiasm” which must be from the beginning the sign of the Prophet. But this enthusiasm is not simply a feeling. It comes from the Prophet's full dedication to God and his mission. (Buber 1985)

Therefore there is nothing strange that the Protestants have, since the 16th century, taught that every believer can interpret God's revelation for himself and that he can also practice it as he himself realizes what is good for him. Thus, the Catholic conception of revelation of the last Church council assumes that God speaks in the Bible through individuals in a personal and human way. However, since God speaks in the Sacred Scripture through men in a human way, the interpreter of the Sacred Scripture, in order to see clearly what God wants to communicate to us, should carefully investigate what the sacred writers really meant, and what God wanted to manifest by the means of their words. To search out the intention of the sacred writers, attention should be paid, among other things, to "literary forms." For truth is set forth and expressed differently in texts which are in different ways of historical, prophetic, poetic nature or of other forms of discourse.

The interpreter must investigate what meaning the sacred writer intended to express and actually expressed in particular circumstances by using contemporary literary forms in accordance with the situation of his own time and culture. For the correct understanding of what the sacred author wanted to assert due attention must be paid to the customary and characteristic styles of feeling, speaking and narrating which prevailed at the time of the sacred writer, and to the patterns that men normally employed at that period in their everyday dealings with one another. (DV 11, 12)

The Holy Spirit not only inspired the biblical writers to have found the right signification of the word, but also monitors the readers of the Bible of all periods and inspires them to find out - in human words of the Bible - God's words. The Holy Spirit, through whom the living voice of the Gospel resounds in the Church and through it in the world, leads unto all truth those who believe and make the word of Christ dwell abundantly in them. (See Col. 3:16 and DV 8)

The origin of the Qur'an is different. It contains only the words that the Archangel Gabriel recited to the Prophet Muhammad, and he repeated them to his disciples. The Bible was written over thousands of years, the Qur'an was completed in a few decades of years, about 35 years after Muhammad's death. Islamic tradition teaches, therefore, that the Archangel Gabriel himself literally dictated the text of the Qur'an to Muhammad. Therefore, the Qur'an should not be interpreted, nor translated, but understood only literally. From the same reason the text of the Qur'an is not explained, except linguistically. Islamic divine revelation has to be understood as it was transmitted. (Lafitte 2006, 81-87)

The core principles here might be expressed in a metaphor. The first version of the basic text of Judaism and Christianity, the Ten Commandments, is one which Jews and Christians no longer have. Even if God himself carved them in a stone, Moses broke the two tablets into pieces. Therefore, he returned to Mount Sinai and, inspired by God, he rewrote the commandments. Thus in Christianity we talk about two authors of the Bible: God and man. Dogmatic constitution on divine revelation says: "In composing the sacred books, God chose men and while employed by Him they made use of their powers and abilities, so that with Him acting in them and through them, they, as true authors, consigned to writing everything and only those things which He wanted." (DV 11) Muslims believe that God's revelation, just as it was revealed to Muhammad is still engraved in a stone in heaven. This idea of Muslims about the origin of revelation is their theological reason for the prohibition of historical, allegorical and other interpretations of the Qur'an. (De Saint-Bon, 2012, 43) This is also the reason for resistance to secularization of Islam. Leaving the daily life and religious debate about principal truths solely to one's own reflection is, in Islam, actually a rebellion against God's revelation. Ignoring the revelation of Qur'an for classical Islam is not secularism, but apostasy from the true faith.

Interpretation of divine revelation in Christianity enables the development of secularization and secularism. Therefore, Christianity can destroy itself.

Conclusion

The Ten Commandments, which are the basic texts of the Judeo Christian tradition, became a part of the values of Western European man. Western democratic society has established respect for the individual and the integrity of his life and his property on one hand but also social solidarity on the other. In the past, Western society has, obviously, via human rights adopted Christian values. But nowadays this society cherishes these values independently of religion. Secularized society maintains that it simply does not need Christianity any more. Furthermore secularism has been transformed into liberalism which strives to liberate itself from the values that have emerged from Christianity and from those practiced by adherents of the religion. This is evident from the examples of the legalization of the termination of unwanted pregnancy, euthanasia and the growing confusion regarding the definition of family. Where the process of liberalism will end no one knows. We may therefore ask: Will the values that Christianity has bestowed on the European culture be able to survive without Christianity? Where will we find transcendence that only allows an absolute ethical stance? We are sure that if there are no ethical criteria (for instance the prohibition not to kill) then people will be able to negotiate for anything that seemingly solves economic problems, even if the price is, for example, the removal of the weak members of the society. We fear that the "abolition" of God is not just the suicide of religion, but also the suicide of civilization. Such a fear is therefore probably justified. The European community would first secularize society and keep Christian values, which it called "human rights," while rejecting the God who is the foundation of Christian values. But what will happen then? Ethics without foundation cannot persist. "Suspension" of God therefore means not only the disappearance of religion, but ultimately leads to the suicide of civilization.

References

Al-Ghanouchi, Rachid, 2000. Secularism in Arab Maghreb. In: John L. Esposito, Azzam Tamini (ed), *Islam and Secularism in the Middle East*. London: Hurst & Company, pp. 97–123.

Ali, Tarik, 2002. *Spopad fundamentalizmov: križarstvo, džihad in modernost*. Ljubljana: Znanstveno in publicistično središče.

DV – 1980, *Dogmatična konstitucija o Božjem razodetju* (*Dogmatic Constitution on Divine Revelation*), Koncilski odloki, Ljubljana.

Buber, Martin. 1985. *La fede dei profeti*. Monferrato: Marietti.

Chadwick, Owen, 1993. *The Secularisation of the European Mind in the 19th Century*. Cambridge: Cambridge University Press.

De Saint-Bon, Henrie. 2012. *L'Islam a la lumier de la foi chretienne*. Paris: l'oeuvre.

ER - *The Encyclopedia of Religion*, Mircea Eliade (ed.), New York: Macmillian Publishing company, vol. 13, 1987.

ERE - Encyclopaedia of Religion and Ethics, Jams Hastings (ed.) Edinburgh: T.and T. Clark, 1954.

Flere Sergej, Kerševan Marko (1995). *Religija in sodobna družba*. Ljubljana: Znanstveno in publicistično središče.

Gauchet, Marcel. 1985. *Le desenchantement du monde*. Paris: Gallimard.

Hervieu-Leger, Daniele. 1993. *La religion pour memoire*. Paris: CERF.

Lafitte, Serge. 2006. *La Bible et le Coran*. Paris: Plon.

LCZ – Leksikon Cankarjeve založbe (1988). Ljubljana: Cankarjeva založba.

Moser, Felix. 1994. *Les croyants non pratiquants*.Geneve: Labor et Fides.

Ocvirk, Drago. 1990. Vidik svetega v osebi in naravi. In: *Nova doba*, Ljubljana: Medškofijski odbor za študente (Družina), pp. 128–151.

Pavel VI. (1976). *O evangelizaciji današnjega sveta*. Ljubljana : Nadškofijski ordinariat.

Poulat, Emile. 1994. *L'ere postchretienne*. Paris: Flammarion.

Sruk Vlado, 1995. *Filozofija*. Ljubljana: Cankarjeva založba.

Štuhec, Ivan. 2012. Sekularizacija kot priložnost za novo religioznost. *Bogoslovni vestnik 72: 55-70.*

Tamini, Azzam, 2000. The Origins of Arab Secularism. In: John L. Esposito, Azzam Tamini (eds.): *Islam and Secularism in the Middle East*. London: Hurst & Company, pp.13–28.

Torres Q., Andres. 2010. Atheism and Christian Images of God. *Concilium* 24: 37–47.

Touraine, Alain. 1992. *Critique de la modernite*. Paris: Fayard.

SUICIDE AND GENOCIDE FROM THE PERSPECTIVE OF IDENTITIES AND NARCISSISM

Erika Prijatelj, *Ljubljana*

1. Identities and violence

YES to life. Among other things this means NO to violence in all its forms. For many people in today's complex and multidimensional world saying *yes to life* leads to confusion and conflict. People are frequently violent toward others and toward themselves, because they are not aware of their own true identity and / or because they are not cognizant regarding the actual identity of others. It is understandable then that people so easily stereotype and compartmentalize themselves and others. Although compartmentalizing life initially appears to be more manageable, in reality, it is more violent and dangerous because of its sectarian and extremist nature. Aggression can be passive or active; it can be expressed internally, externally or both.

The answer to the question of who we really are deeply marks our relationship with ourselves and with others. Indeed, this answer contains the key of our relationship to life and death. Oscar Wilde (2007, 39) at the end of the 19th century stated that most people are considered to be really "other people". By identifying themselves with someone else, their thinking and feelings become the opinions and feelings of others. Living results in imitating their models, idols or leaders, while their actual desires and needs, originality and wounds remain an undiscovered planet to themselves and others. Living with a false identity in adulthood - the period of assuming full responsibility for oneself – engenders psychological and spiritual suicide.

We are strongly influenced by people with whom we identify and in addition to other powers they can easily transfer aversion and hostile feelings. Without a clearly defined personal identity we are unable to recognize the lethalness of these kinds of negative feelings and vibrations and consequently we cannot resist them. The former Yugoslavia, Rwanda, Israel, Palestine, Iraq, Sudan, Syria and other parts of the world provide many examples of such identifications. These phenomena are also present in the Church. Identification with a group, which submits to baiting, results in *borrowed identity people* expanding with the speed of fire transforming themselves into a powerful weapon of brutality and an implementation of genocide against others.

Identity has the capacity to kill. This occurs when a strong, exclusive sense of belonging to a group exists accompanied by a belief that others are very different, wrong or even foreign, hostile or threatening. Thus, we are no longer Christians, but Catholics and Protestants; Catholic Charismatic Renewal and ordinary parishioners; Opus Dei and its opponents. "It appears that cultivated violence associated with identity conflicts, increases steadily throughout the world" (Sen,

2006, 3) on the racial, ethnic, religious level and on the level of other selective loyalties which with their exaggerations lead to violence toward other groups.

It is much too simple to say that all people are more or less the same. Monochromatic perception of the world and viewing it as a collection of religions and cultures or civilizations and cultures overlooks the immense plurality and richness of human identity, based on different values: morality, sex, ethnicity, communication, education, language, politics, personal and societal history, spirituality, science, economics, etc. and a unique relationship between the various aspects. The quest for peace, for instance, can bind people whose starting point is the example of Christ, new age music or political multiculturalism, religious fundamentalism or the fight against global terrorism, postcolonial history or many other incentives.

Hasty and superficial classification of people is in itself violent because people recognize themselves as members of different groups, and at the same time they belong to these groups. These groups can be a primary family, nationality, religion, geographical origin, language, dialect, status, age, profession, work, love for a certain type of art, eating, recreational habits and many more. We are significantly shaped by each of these groups, which enables the development of a specific aspect of our personal identity, and therefore we can never be limited to one 'drawer'. To believe that a person has only one identity is an illusion. Excessive focus on one aspect of an individual's identity is misleading and destructive. Viewing others or ourselves in this manner is disruptive even if this considering is an excessive exaltation of one identity over the other. Very often it is an expression of narcissism and its related aggression.

2. Forms of narcissism

We live in an "age of the relentless rise of narcissism in our culture" (Tweng and Campbell, 2009, 26). This is a phenomenon of the Western world, which is reflected in the education of children, when they are indulged and do whatever they wish. In adults this is evidenced by the preoccupation with individual self-fulfillment and pursuing a lifestyle that separates a person from the community. Regarding the issue of human identity it is necessary to distinguish between healthy narcissism and an unhealthy narcissistic personality disorder. Today the latter is increasingly pronounced. Healthy narcissism is expressed by "self-esteem, realistic self-evaluation, quality of work and genuine love" (Sperry 2011, 174). Pathological narcissism is manifested by arrogance and is conveyed as superiority over others. Common to all forms of unhealthy narcissism is a non-acceptance of oneself and consequently an inauthentic identity.

Pathological narcissism is revealed in a variety of forms. It may be overt, covert or malignant. Classic narcissism is overt and is manifested as exhibitionism. Overt narcissists consider themselves to be better than others, they constantly seek attention, they lack emotional warmth and are unable to sustain loving relationships. They maintain excessive concern for their status, power and property and they are preoccupied with their appearance. They have an excessively high opinion of themselves, have little awareness of their own weaknesses and of the needs of others. Subsequently, they lack the ability to empathize. When others surpass them in their field of expertise, overt narcissists react with despondency, depression, shame and jealousy. When rejection and opposition are experienced these emotions are intensified. At that time, because of insecurity, they frequently react ferociously, which is expressed by rage, verbal insults as well as hostile behavior. Overt narcissists are consumed with comparing themselves with others and expend significant energy on justifying their wounded self-esteem. This is achieved through self-idealization and devaluation of others. When they idealize someone, they feel more important because of the link they have with the idealized person and when they humiliate someone they feel stronger than the one humiliated. In summary, the overt narcissist places all others in one of three 'compartments': other people feeling unreasonably idealized, unreasonably demeaned or simply not taken into account.

As opposed to overt narcissists covert narcissists often exercise exaggerated restraint and present as very attentive to the needs of others. Covert narcissists give both the appearance of humility as well as the impression that they do not desire to be the center of attention. However, they are "tremendously sensitive to criticism, indifference and underestimation by others" (Masterson 1993, 64). Similar to overt narcissists covert narcissists maintain arrogant fantasies, are very sensitive to their perceived rights and can also be exploitative. Under stress they assume a defensive posture, become hostile and prone to self-reproaches. They struggle not only with the thought that they are not able to realize their dreams but also with feelings of guilt when they become aware of their competitive, exhibitionistic and aggressive cravings, which can lead to suppression of their awareness. Despite believing that they deserve recognition for their uniqueness, in reality, covert narcissists struggle with doubts about themselves and therefore do not seek the direct approval of others. Fear of exposure often prevents them from entering into intimate relationships. Instead they are drawn to the company of people where they feel inferior. When praise is received they view it as insincere and are then faced with the fear that they will not be able to meet the task. This fear can lead to flattering others, people whose successes they actually envy and toward whom they innerly harbor resentment and contempt. Due to unfulfilled expectations their mood is marked by a disguised anger and vacillates between irritability and depression, which then can develop into vengeance or maliciousness. Their attention to others is not a sign of empathy.

Malignant narcissism is the most hostile form of narcissism. In addition to the features of overt narcissism, this form expresses "sadistic, paranoid, antisocial or psychopathic characteristics" (Šlosar, 2009, 22), which may reach genocidal proportions. Malignant narcissists present as self-sufficient and successful people although they experience themselves as fragile and vulnerable when exposed to insults. They are overly sensitive to criticism. Failure in endeavors results in feelings of emptiness, irritability, revenge, suspicion and sadistic aggression. When not engaged in their narcissistic pursuits they are cold, non-empathetic, exploitative and indifferent to the needs and feelings of others.

In today's western world, which strongly supports individualism and various forms of self-fulfillment, pathological narcissism as well as the associated violence toward ourselves and others emerge as a normal way of living. Ronningstam (2011, 216) in her recent book pointed out that it is necessary when studying people distressed by pathological narcissism, to see not only their haughtiness, ambition or their grandiose desire to be something more than they are or somebody they are not, but also their vulnerability.

Because self-centered people feel unprotected and insecure they have difficulty coping with their vulnerability and fragility. Criticism from their environment results in disproportionately deep suffering and provokes in them a defensive or offensive stance. Under these circumstances suicidal ideation may develop in all forms of pathological narcissism; however, the risk is more pronounced in the case of covert narcissism.

When people are admired and exalted above others they are not necessarily loved. Happily belonging to someone does not require personal perfection. The key is mutual love, which implies acceptance of oneself and the other, thus leading to the recognition and acceptance of one's own fragility and the fragility of the other.

3. Narcissism and suicide

People who commit or attempt to commit suicide, are commonly seen as depressed and miserable, who experience a loss of pleasure and interest. Such people are also viewed as tired, having low concentration, people who often struggle with feelings of despair and guilt as well as serious mental patients. Yet, it is not necessary that narcissistic people are prone to depression; on the contrary, they can be very active and effective with a strong sense of reality. The dynamic arises from the pathological glorification of themselves. This is accompanied by narcissistic vulnerability and fear either of subordination or feelings of loss and inferiority. Their dynamic focuses primarily on the protection of their glorious self-image.

The dynamic of narcissistic people with suicidal tendencies has several features. Initially, suicidal ideation can artificially raise their self-esteem as it supports the illusion of power and control, for example: "I'm not afraid of anything, not even of death." Secondly, suicidal behavior can be a defense against an anticipated threat or suffering as in: "I'd rather die than have to endure such shame." Thirdly, suicidal initiative can arise from an individual's aggressive, vengeful and controlling attitude, such as: "Either my way or no way" or "I'll show you!"

Fourthly, stemming from the belief in one's sublime indestructibility, one predicates: "I'm not like the others. Nothing bad will happen to me." Fifthly, suicidal ideation can express a desire to destroy an imperfect, weak and unmaintainable self. These attitudes may occur in complex combinations, for instance: "I will destroy my body in order to save my perfect soul" or "If I kill myself before I am exposed by the shame I will be seen as perfect and I have all things under control." But above all, the central motive for suicide stems from the illusion that the person will transform a passive humiliation into an active control of the situation and into a victory over fear, pain or death (Ronningstam 2005, 159-180).

Two fundamental types of suicide in conjunction with narcissistic disorder can be detected in the above five examples. The first is metamorphic suicide, which is based on the fantasy that suicide is an act of transformation from an unsustainable present to a better future. This type of suicide occurs in people whose grandiosity and cruelty have risen to malignant proportions. It reflects a realistic perception of a confused self, a self that holds disharmonious different aspects of self-identities, which are in constant flux. The second type, executive suicide, is one in which ideation becomes a practice. In an attempt to free the good self from the bad self the superego attacks the unacceptable and unbearable body.

Narcissistic people often reflect their original identification with the sadistic objectivized image of others. In many cases this image is a product of the internalized negative and punitive childhood experiences of others. In practice it appears in patterns of revenge and control. From the perspective of the human self's identities narcissistic people, because of their unstable self-image, deepen the split between the bodily and other identities. They objectify their body allowing an abnormal risk of physical and aggressive attack, which can end in suicide. In a therapeutic relationship self-destructive and suicidal behavior can also be employed as a means of establishing and maintaining power over the therapist.

To question from the perspective of narcissism whether there is a link between suicide and genocide, we need only to remember A. Hitler, who in Europe and the world was responsible for millions of deaths and who in the end committed suicide. Was Hitler with his killings a monster? Not at all. Hitler was a person who among other things suffered from strong pathological narcissism. He was elected by people who needed an influential leader to realize their dreams.

4. Beyond the boundaries of executive identity

The main causes of suicide among Slovenes are cultural-historical and increasingly socio-economic ones. The causes are influenced by Slovenian values and habits, patterns of education and communication as well as the presence of a broader context, which contributes to the development of discordant identities and split personalities. Employing a psychoanalytic vocabulary Slovenians can be described as anankastic, depressed and inclined to frenetic productivity. Therefore, very pronounced in the foreground is the executive identity. Suicidal tendencies can be triggered by loss of one's reputation, failure, rejection or disapproval by a significant authority, person or institution, loss of property etc., all of which have a strong negative effect on feelings of self-worth.

In general Slovenians do not know how to express their feelings and dreams, to talk personally, to negotiate constructively, to collaborate and to enjoy the success of their neighbors or peers without jealousy. They frequently vacillate between 'all or nothing', which is one of the characteristics of narcissistic personalities. When the suppressed issues in them become too large and too heavy, Slovenians become violent and the lightning conductor of this violence is their own body and / or other people.

Within the context of human identities the executive identity has its unique place. A problem arises when the executive identity is allowed to dominate the others: physical, spiritual, individual, psychosocial and psychosexual identity - and when a person is seen and appreciated only in the light of productivity, status and appearance. Executive identity easily embraces the logic of economy and capitalism, but it does not accommodate the deeper issues as: the meaning of life, love, relationships, gratuity and transcendence; executive identity fails to respect people in their uniqueness and their ability to create not only for profit. For all of this the executive identity lacks a moral imagination, which is based on a person's authentic self and inner integrity. Striving for authenticity and integrity is the path from narcissism and the way to living a meaningful and fulfilling life.

Moral imagination develops the capacity to perceive things beyond what is initially seen. It is an awareness of ourselves and others on a deeper level. Metaphorically speaking, it is the light that illuminates the mystery, hidden behind human executive identity and every visible reality. It could be called the power of seeing the very essence of things and relationships.The Future enters into us assisted by moral imagination and is transformed within us before it comes to be. Imagination is necessary for every creative activity and for the future of humanity. To not only exist, but to live fully in this broken world, a healthy imagination is needed. Imagination has creative and artistic features. New things come into existence and the old ones are transformed. "Moral imagination encourages the discovery of new ways of seeing, hearing, feeling, thinking, contemplating, being close, belonging" (Lederach 2005, 153) and this is our transformation.

Moral imagination has a quality of transcendence, and therefore it is not imprisoned in narrowness, prejudices nor in cultural and structural constraints. It rejects narcissistic as well as fixed views and responses and dares to take risks and create new spaces and new relationships, thus opening the way to a new community - a new human family. Moral imagination offers opportunities that cannot be imagined within the existing frameworks. From isolation and narcissistic attitudes or experiences of domination moral imagination inspires us toward a vision of interdependent relationships, which also includes our rivals and enemies.Creativity is therefore the art of creating something, which does not yet exist, and of giving it life. According to Einstein, logic leads us from A to B, while moral imagination is capable of leading us everywhere. By everywhere is meant the area of boundless respect for our own life and for the life of every other person, acceptance of vulnerabilities and maintaining the courage to risk entering into the unknown with people whom we least understand or fear the most - even when we are most afraid of ourselves.

Conclusion

No one is an island. Belonging to different groups, which for each person depends on one's specific life context, is very important for human existence. *Yes to life* requires the choice of belonging to someone or something. Without belonging a person experiences a feeling of a bitter senselessness. Therefore the ability to give or find meaning in one's own life and in the lives of others becomes radically threatened. However, a person encounters a unique challenge when competitiveness enters into his/her belonging to various groups or communities. Competition is a signal that an internal conflict exists between different identities and priorities, each of which in their own way requires loyalty. A person is then faced with a decision regarding which are more or less important. Finally, this choice is highly dependent on the context of one's life.

In this discernment it is necessary to be mindful of two important aspects (Sen 2006, 19). First, human self-identity contains specifically different identities; therefore, they always exist in the plural. The importance of any one identity per se does not reduce the importance of the others. Second, a person is faced with a choice, which can be either explicit or implicit. It depends on the level of importance that a person gives to each single identity, the degree of loyalty toward each identity and on one's relationship toward all other identities as a whole. This type of choice does not mean to ignore the loyalty to all others, which for a person are less important identities. However, if a person ignores this loyalty, more tension is created both in the individual and in society, which subsequently produces conflicts and violence toward oneself and the others, as in suicide and genocide. Likewise, the choice of the identity does not depreciate but confirms that people have many common identities and that life is not simply black and white.

An example of a free and clear, although difficult choice is M. Gandhi, who gave priority to his identification with the Indian people, who were striving for independence from British rule, before consideration of his identity as qualified lawyer who endeavored to achieve justice in the English legal system. Another example is E. Forster (1951, 42), who stated: "If I had to choose between betraying my county and betraying my friend, I hope I will have the courage to betray my county." Such a choice is possible only by a genuine person acting within a free reflection, which is able to set priorities. An illusion of identity is the opposite, as was demonstrated during the presentation of pathological narcissism, which disables us from any complex discernment of multidimensional reality and from taking responsibility for our decisions. In dilemmas the choices include giving up the dissimilarities and require a "genuine moral weighing of the situation" (Taylor 2007, 479) employing much moral imagination.

Today it is necessary to deal not only with the problems of economics and the politics of globalization, but primarily with issues of values, ethics and a sense of belonging, which shape our understanding not only of ourselves but also of the broader world. The narcissistic vision is actually not a vision but an illusion. Narcissistic individuals and groups of narcissistic people support the vision of isolated horseback riders who care only for their own welfare. In the long term they do not contribute to a full understanding and shaping of human identity capable of transcending a painful past and an insecure present. The more the world feels threatened and where more narcissistic motives prevail, the greater is the risk for more suicides and new genocides. The world today urgently needs a healthy moral imagination with which to envision a different, but accessible world, in which many common identities will be recognized and mutual differences will be respected, a world in which success will be redefined and where we will live in genuine solidarity.

References

Foster, Edward M. 1951. *Two Cheers for Democracy.* London: Arnold.

Lederach, John Paul. 2005. *The Moral Imagination: The Art and Soul of Building Peace.* Oxford: Oxford University Press.

Masterson, James F. 1993. *The Emerging Self: A Developmental Self and Object Relations Approach to the Treatment of the Closet Narcissistic Disorder of the Self.* New York: Brunner/Mazel Publishers.

Ronningstam, Elsa F. 2011. Narcissistic Personality Disorder in DSM. In: In Support of Retaining a Significant Diagnosis. *Journal of Personality Disorders,* 25(2): 248–259.

Ronningstam, Elsa F. 2005. *Identifyng and Understanding the Narcissistic Personality.* Oxford: Oxford University Press.

Sen, Amartya. 2006. *Identity and Violence: The Illusion of Destiny.* New York: W.W. Norton.

Sperry, Len and Sperry, Jon. 2011. Healthy Narcissism and Narcissistic Personality Disorder. *Human Development, 32*(4): 5–16.

Šlosar, Jay R. 2009. *The Culture of Excess.* Santa Barbara, CA: Praeger.

Taylor, Charles. 2007. *A Secular Age.* Cambridge, MA: Belknap/Harvard University Press.

Twenge, Jean W. and Campbell, K. 2009. *The Narcissism Epidemic: Living in the Age of Entitlement.* New York: Free Press, a division of Simon & Schuster.

Wilde, Oscar. 2007. *De Profundis.* New York: Book Jungle Publisher.

FACING SUICIDE AND GENOCIDE: EDUCATIONAL CHALLENGES

Stanko Gerjolj, *Ljubljana*

Regarding suicide, Slovenia is ranked among the top three European countries, the only two countries ahead of Slovenia are Hungary and Latvia (Kalin 2012). It is worth noting that suicide is a both a European problem and, more generally, an issue of so-called high-tech societies, which use the results of scientific progress not only in the service of life, but also for its endangering and (self-) destruction. In addition to the use of knowledge in the service of violence, suicide is reflected in the way modern man resolves the issues of the beginning and end of earthly life. If we compare the number of births to the number of abortions, it is difficult for us to say that adults communicate to young people genuine respect and joy for life (Škedelj et al. 2011, 207). Some environments also reveal similar trends in dilemmas of euthanasia. The issues of suicide and genocide also fall within this context.

Genocide and suicide in the Bible

The Bible does not speak of 'suicide' directly, but talks about the actions of individuals and groups that contain dimensions of both suicide as well as genocide.

The most famous suicide is that committed by Judas Iscariot, who betrayed Jesus and then hanged himself (Mt 27.5).[1] While did Peter disown Jesus, he did so out of fear and not so intentionally as Judas. When he discovers his weakness in fear, he repents and becomes a key character in salvation history of Jesus. In contrast, Judas is far too infatuated with himself and his intentions to ask for forgiveness. Although his betrayal is also part of God's plan (Matjaž 2004, 105) this does not reduce the gravity of his action. Immediately after betrayal, he distances himself from the apostles and isolates himself, and tries to solve his distress by himself, by trying to return the 'death' money back to legal representatives who cannot provide him with absolution (Arko 2013, 121). As he becomes impenitent before a merciful God, he is no longer able to accept or tolerate himself. Trapped in sin and feeling of his own shame, he is frightened of himself. As he is no longer capable of either interpersonal or religious communication,

[1] Some authors believe that Matthew, when describing Judah's suicide, leaned on the below-mentioned Ahithopfel who also hung himself (Arko 2013, 123) and even allow the possibility that it is a fictional character, but given the fact that is being mentioned by all evangelists and that he is known by the Christian tradition from the beginning, this is not likely (Brown 1998, 1394–1395).

the only thing he sees in his desperation is suicide, with which he also betrays himself.

Some form of (self-) destructive tendencies can already be traced back to the biblical report of the Flood. Noah with his family is saved from this crisis. Those who are saved are people who are open to communication with God. In addition to these, Noah invites those beings to his ark who are capable of natural relationships, so he calls them in pairs – male and female (Gen 7.1–5).

Another example of being trapped in the destruction of life can be found in the report on Sodom and Gomorrah. Even from this devastating crisis, the only one who is saved with the help of God and Abraham is Lot with his family. Abraham's negotiating with God proves that a 'civilization of death' cannot be changed unless people are willing to actively participate. The only ones who can be saved are individuals and small communities who are able to leave the cultural death and rise to the level of life – in the natural environment of the mountains to which Lot's family is headed. However, his wife does not reach the safe environment because she 'looked back longingly and was turned into a pillar of salt' (Gen 19.26). Clearly, any flirting with one's misguided past is dangerous and leads to unnatural and premature death.

Samson's suicide is interesting from a modern perspective, which has – except for the biblical theological context – some parallels with Islamic suicidal acts with genocidal additions (Jdg 16.23-31). With Samson's suicide, the period of the judges also ends, with which the Bible announces that genocidal and suicidal actions and revenge from even 'noble' motives have no acceptance even in the eyes of God (Bible 2001, 321).

Saul's suicide attempt [2] is interesting in the fact that it triggers a chain reaction, because in addition to him, this action is also performed by his shield-bearers, who had previously refused Saul's request to kill him (1 Sam 31.4–6). In a slightly different but comparable circumstances king of Israel, Zimri, commits suicide by self-immolation; he first came to power through a military coup and then committed mass murder against his political competitors (1 Chr 16.5–20). It is worth noting that they also came to a 'dead end' and did 'what was evil in the eyes of the Lord' (1 Chr 15.34). Zimri was no different; when he was distressed due to repeated military coups, he took his own life. In a similar situation, David's treacherous adviser Ahithophel (2 Sam 17.23) hangs himself. Thus, the Bible describes in a vivid way how moving away from God degrades the system of ethical and moral values and develops a 'culture of death', in

[2] In the second book of Samuel, we find that Saul's suicide was unsuccessful and that he was only put to death upon his request by an Amalekite who happened to pass by (2 Sam 1.6–10). Given the signs that Saul was already severely wounded before his suicide attempt, some authors associate his action more with euthanasia than with a conventional suicide (Rosner 1997, 275).

which both those who initiate the process of devaluation of life as well as those who repeat these mistakes compulsively lose or take their lives.

The second book of Maccabees tells the story of two suicides that carry a slightly different message. Both cases are about the deliberate creating of circumstances and pressures that bring two benevolent and innocent people into desperate situations, where they saw death as the only solution. In the first, Ptolomeus, nicknamed Makron, (despite his generous efforts for justice, his intentions were not perfectly noble) took his own life with poison due to loss of a reputable job (2 Mkb 10.13). The case of Razis is about martyr's death and not suicide (2 Mkb 14.37–46). He was an extremely good and honest man, one of the elders of Jerusalem, even called 'the father of the Jews' due to his nobility (2 Mkb 14.37) who became a means of achieving political goals, in this case, an expression of hatred towards Jews. He preferred 'an honourable death' over unfair abduction (2 Mkb 14.42), so in the last moment he rushes into death, which (in communication with God) he reaches only in the third step: at first, he stabbed himself; next, threw himself of the city walls; then, ran to a jagged rock, where he 'tore out his insides with both hands and threw them down at people', while praying aloud, 'Lord of life and breath, I trust you to give these back to me' (2 Mkb 14.46).

At the same time, the Old Testament provides several examples of a righteous man in distress, desiring death. A good example is Job, who illustrates the dramatic dynamics of the personal growth of a man experiencing painful changes and losing on his way (Corey 1995, 44). In extremely perilous circumstances, the only thing that keeps him alive is in-depth communication with God, which helps him to rise above the loss and the pain that have changed him, and led him to the mature and integrated age (Whitehead & Whitehead 1990, 65). Even Sarah, the daughter of Raguel from the Book of Tobit plans her suicide and wants to hang herself, but at the end changes her decision for the love of her father (Tob 3.10) and seeks help from God in her prayer (Tob 3.11–13).

The Bible sees suicide mostly as a consequence of distancing oneself from God, sinfulness and 'wrong paths' for people who are not willing or able to admit their missteps, repent of them and be transformed. A sinner who repents and becomes converted shall receive God's mercy, and in most cases also human understanding. However, anyone who sees only himself and shuts himself in his own impenitence cannot find a way out of distress and has no other choice than to take his own life.

Why is Moses forbidden from going into the Promised Land?

God describes the reasons for the prohibition of Moses entry into the Promised Land as 'misbelief' and 'infidelity', which he detected in some of the key steps of his mission (Nu Mz 20.10–13; Dt 32.48–52). In the context of Moses's biography, the Promised Land represents a synonym for the meaning of life, which can be attained only after death, when we see God 'face to face' (1 Cor 13.12). The Promised Land is presented to us as the final objective, which we can perceive only as it is receding from us, and is much more of a path than an objective (Ex 33.22–23).

To achieve meaning in life probably means achieving anything that is worth living for. When a man reaches this ultimate meaning of earthly life, based on common sense, he runs out of arguments for life, and in the event that this feeling really comes upon him, death is the next logical step. This way – thank God – the meaning of life keeps evading us and we can continually look for it. It is actually not so much about evading us in the negative sense of the word. It is rather more about an attractive God's 'flirting' with a man, watching with a mirror, which awakens the desire looking at someone face to face. The ultimate meaning of life is not a human right, but a gift of God, which we keep chasing throughout the healthy game of life, and in the end it approaches us on its own (Koenig 1992, 115–116). We can anticipate it just enough that we cannot follow it – until death, when we see the Promised Land, and we enter it only through the door of death.

Similarly as we cannot see God 'face to face', because looking for him is something we need, which – if this is done sincerely and with dedication – includes a doubt, we also cannot find or achieve the meaning of life. We are always at the 'gap of present time'; on looking back to the past, we recognize the soundness, beauty and fullness of life and draw existential power from it, but when looking into the future we look at the meaning into his 'back' and follow it persistently, although we cannot catch or realize it 'in pieces'.

The fact the Promised Land is moving away from our death can be anticipated in a conversation with any older man, when he sometimes suggests plans for the future that surpass any realistic possibilities. Upon due consideration, he is also aware he will not reach them, but needs them and carries them within him as he draws strength and motivation from them for smaller, completely realistic and everyday plans. He probably feels that without such big plans he would grow careless and slovenly, and would not be able to perform most urgent everyday tasks and errands. When the end to earthly life is approached, which a man can sense and feel, his objectives are increasingly trapped in the current experience and semiconscious 'daydreaming', but this is still a communication that prevents resignation regarding life, and is also in the ultimate part of earthly life a sign of integration (Loder 1998, 321). Thus, this moving away from the Promised Land motivates us to avoid death, but to dedicate ourselves to life in such difficult moments (Meier 1988, 119). In this, 'daydreaming' time represents a multi-faceted dimension and also includes the emotional dimension of life, which allows the very avoidance of the final objective. Therefore, it is good not to know the date when our last looking into the Promised Land will change into living in it, as knowing such information would only burden us (Meier 1988,

125). The prohibition of Moses from entering the Promised Land, therefore, is first of all not a punishment for doubt and infidelity, but primarily a gift of God that gives meaning to life until the end of time on earth.

A multi-faceted dimension is also discovered in the composition of Pentateuch, which represents a unique whole. The Pentateuch of Moses does not end with a report of entry into the Promised Land, but the final chapters are still intended for our preparation to enter this land. Likewise, in the last chapter, God in talking to Moses, where he announces that his earthly life will end before entering the Promised Land, for the last time refers to the patriarchs Abraham, Isaac and Jacob and this way reasonably brings together the given promise with Moses to them (Friedman 2001, 677). With Moses, namely, he brings it to the door of eternity and there, on the mountain 'Heaven', – by looking into the Promised Land – ends any healthy and reasonable human life of earth.

Education for Life

In accordance with the story of Moses, we find that man lives as long as he can yearn for the 'Promised Land'. The longing is significantly related to the ability to set objectives. Particularly in late middle and older periods of life, when suicides are most frequent,[3] objectives can also be associated with the religious dimension of life, not least by prayer. The value of religion as a stabilizing factor is confirmed both by the statistical data regarding suicide (Bertolote & Fleischmann 2002, 8) as well as by psychologists and psychotherapists (Meves 2008; Gams 2005, 44; Musek 2005, 50). Many researchers recognize that involvement in a religious community, particularly in relation to depression, is inversely proportional to the number of suicides (Židanik 47). Moreover, the fact that there are much more suicides committed by men than women (Vertot 2010) is another confirmation, because women are generally more active in religious communities, although the stated difference, of course, has other reasons. It is important in religious education that a positive image of loving God is communicated to children and young people (Košir 1999, 4–5), which is possible only with mutually understanding, respectful and loving parents (Gostečnik 2005, 158).

In modern society, the existential emptiness and the related apathy are the main elements that threaten life and push people into feelings of purposeless (Blasco–Fontecilla et al. 2013, 23; Zalokar Divjak 2000, 121). These feelings are often the result of a lack of common values and the fact that young people are often spoiled. This is often associated with unsafe and broken family relationships, which nevertheless are the primary living space both for young and adults (Braconnier 2001, 280). Specifically, an environment in which the value of sincere

[3] In Slovenia, suicide is increasing; the most threatened generation is those older than 65, slightly less so those between the ages of 50 and 64 and even less between the ages of 35 and 49; the rate is decreasing in the latter two groups (Kalin 2012).

and genuine and lasting and loyal relationships is lost, while at the same time creating a 'culture' of painful circumvention, represents the fundamental living space as extremely dangerous and unworthy of trust to a child. This 'game' often includes children who are on the one hand overwhelmed by pain of parents and bereft of genuine and sincere relations (Kompan Erzar 2003, 37, 50), while spoiled on the other. When children and young people have their needs met too quickly, they easily lose motivation to work and live and find themselves in an existential vacuum, in which they start making attempts on their own lives. When children do not need to make effort to achieve their goals, they lose their will, motivation and become completely non-resistant (Žorž 2002, 84).

In this context, challenges emerge for education at three levels: at the level of forming common values, at the level of sensitizing people for the religious dimension of life, and at the level of efforts for secure and lasting relationships.

Society needs solid common and enduring values that are not based purely in the self, but which inspire and motivate a person, particularly in the other and Other (Juhant 2006, 33). This is, of course, filled with meaning and changes more myself than the other towards a more integrated person (Vodičar 2006, 297).[4]

Despite liberalization, contemporary society shows signals of an in-depth reflection of life that longs for ultimate meaning, and such holistic considerations often perceive how common values with the 'moral imperative' at least indirectly relate to the religious dimension (Klun 2006, 92–93; Jamnik 2006, 81), particularly in the existential sense (Petkovšek 2007, 127–128). As regards the issues of meaning, existential approach and biographical learning are more important factors than empirical evidence and 'mathematical' logic (Roebben 2011, 89).

In addition to exercising common values and the religious dimension of life, the need for safe and healthy relationships or families can be observed. At all three levels, the Church feels called to creative collaboration (Meves 2008, 179). In accordance with tradition, the Church is also called to curative, in some sense even therapeutic action, where it firstly sees a man in distress and is then able, in the process of healing, to properly change also the environment, which provides both for individual as well as for community, a type of existence more worthy of human beings (Barragan 2006, 20). It is worth noting that the Church is not only a social institution but a community of 'faith and hope' permanently reflecting its functioning through the last sense of transcendental life (Baloban 2007, 198). Only this fact gives a person in distress that hope, which the 'world' is unable to give (2 Tim 3.15).

[4] Moses drew motivation for his mission distinctively in 'others' and repeatedly strengthened it in communication with God, while mostly changing himself, which led him to a meaningful conclusion of the earthly life.

Biblical characters acted in no easier circumstances than those typical for contemporary times and let us know, through their actions, that the 'pedagogy of hoping relationships' is always possible. However, it does not depend primarily on material well-being but on sincere searching for the truth and Truth, and sincere and genuine as well as sentient and respectful communication at all levels – both in the Church as well as in wider society.

References

Arko, Andraž. 2013. *Edukativna razsežnost in katehetsko-pastoralna uporabnost filma Kristusov pasijon režiserja Mela Gibsona.* Doktorska disertacija. Teološka fakulteta Univerze v Ljubljani.

Baloban, Josip. 2007. Christsein und Kirche im Dialog mit der Transformationsgesellschaft. In: P. Hünermann & J. Juhant & B. Žalec (eds). *Dialogue and Virtue. Ways to Overcome Clashes of Our Civilizations.* Berlin: Lit, 191–202.

Bertolote, M. Jose & Fleischmann, Alexandra. 2002. A global perspective in the epidemiology of suicide. *Suicidology*, 7(2): 6–8. http://iasp.info/pdf/papers/Bertolote.pdf (accessed July 20st 2013).

Blasco-Fontecilla, Hilario & de León-Martínez, Victoria & Delgado-Gomez, David & Giner, Lucas & Guillaume, Sebastien & Courtet, Philippe. 2013. Emptiness and suicidal behavior: an exploratory review. *Suicidology Online*, 4: 21–32. http://www.suicidology-online.com/pdf/SOL-2013-4-21-32.pdf (accessed July 20st 2013).

Braconnier, Alain. 2001. *Kako razumeti mladostnika.*Tržič: Učila.

Brown E. Raymond. 1998. *The Death of the Messiah.* New York: Doubleday.

Corey, A. Michael. 1995. *Job, Jonah and the Unconscious: A Psychological Interpretation of Evil and Spiritual Growth in the Old Testament.* Lanham–New York–London: University Press of America.

Friedman, R. Elliott. 2001. *Commentary on the Torah: With a New English Translation.* San Francisco: Harper Collins Publishers.

Gostečnik, Christian. 2005. *Psihoanaliza in religiozno izkustvo.* Ljubljana: Brat Frančišek in Frančiškanski družinski Inštitut.

Gams, Matjaž. (2005). Znanost o verovanju. *Informacijska družba IS 2005: Zbornik 8. mednarodne multikonference.* Ljubljana: Institut 'Jožef Stefan', 43–47.

Jamnik, Anton. 2006. A Person between Rawls' (liberalistic) procedural Justice and the Communitarian Good. J. Juhant & B. Žalec (eds). *Person and Good: Man and His Ethics in the Postmodern World.* Berlin: Lit, 65–82.

Juhant, Janez. 2006. Autonomous Person as the Basis of Ethics: Man between modern and postmodern morality. J. Juhant & B. Žalec (eds). *Person and Good: Man and His Ethics in the Postmodern World.* Berlin: Lit, 17–35.

Kalin, Katja. 2012. Svetovni dan preprečevanja samomora. *Statistični urad Republike Slovenije.* 7. september 2012. http://www.stat.si/novica_prikazi.aspx?id=4953 (accessed July 20st 2013).

Klun, Branko. 2006. Der Anspruch des Anderen: Überlegungen zum "postmodernen" Guten. J. Juhant & B. Žalec (eds). *Person and Good: Man and His Ethics in the Postmodern World.* Berlin: Lit, 83–94.

Koenig, G. Harold. 1992. Religion and Prevention of Illness in Later Life. Pargament I. Kenneth & Maton I. Kenneth & Robert E. Hess (eds). *Religion and Prevention in*

Mental Health: Research, Vision, and Action. New York – London – Norwood: The Haworth Press, 105–125.

Kompan Erzar, L. Katarina. 2003. *Skrita moč družine*. Ljubljana: Brat Frančišek in Frančiškanski družinski Inštitut.

Košir, Katja. 1999. Zakaj na dveh bregovih? *Panika*, št. 3. Ljubljana: DŠPS, 4–7.

Loder, E. James. 1998. *The Logic of the Spirit: Human Development in Theological Perspective*. San Francisco: Jossey-Bass Publishers.

Matjaž, Maksimilijan. 2004. *Eksegeza Nove zaveze – Markov evangelij*. Ljubljana: Teološka fakulteta.

Meier, Levi. 1988. *Jewish Values in Psychotherapy: Essays on Vital Issues on the Search for Meaning*. Lanham: University Press of America.

Meves, Christa. 2008. *Zapeljani. Zlorabljeni. Izigrani*. Celje: Celjska Mohorjeva družba.

Musek, Janek. 2005. Psihološki, nevroznanstveni in evolucijski vidiki verskega doživljanja. *Informacijska družba IS 2005: Zbornik 8. mednarodne multikonference*. Ljubljana: Institut 'Jožef Stefan', 48–51.

Petkovšek, Robert. 2007. Glaubenswissen. J. Juhant & B. Žalec (eds). *On Cultivating Faith and Science: Reflections on Two Key Topics of Modern Ethics*. Berlin: Lit, 121–133.

Roebben, Bert. 2011. *Religionspädagogik der Hoffnung: Grundlinien religiöser Bildung in der Spätmoderne*. Berlin: Lit.

Rosner, Fred. 1997. *Medicine in the Bible and the Talmud: Selections from Classical Jewish Sources*. Hoboken NJ: KTAV Publishing House.

Sveto pismo Stare in Nove zaveze. 2001. Ljubljana: Svetopisemska družba Slovenije.

Škedelj, Meta & Markovič, Eva & Vatovec, Neža. 2011. *Labirint kot metoda v službi edukacije za osebnostno rast*. Diplomsko delo. Teološka fakulteta Univerze v Ljubljani.

Vertot, Nelka. 2010. Svetovni dan preprečevanja samomora. *Statistični urad Republike Slovenije*. 8. september 2010. http://www.stat.si/novica_prikazi.aspx?id=3380 (accessed July 20st 2013).

Vodičar, Janez. 2006. Selbsterziehung als Weg zur Person. J. Juhant & B. Žalec (eds). *Person and Good: Man and His Etchics in the Postmodern World*. Berlin: Lit, 293–308

Whitehead, E. Evelyn & Whitehead, D. James. 1990. *Les étapes de l'âge adulte*. Paris: Centurion.

Zalokar Divjak, Zdenka. 2000. *Vzgajati z ljubeznijo*. Krško: Gora.

Židanik, Suzana. 2005. Religija in odnos do zdravja in zdravljenja. Družinska medicina na stičišču kultur, 45–55. Http://stari.drmed.org/index.php?k=3&n=73 (accessed July 21st 2013).

Žorž, Bogdan. 2002. *Razvajenost: rak sodobne vzgoje*. Celje: Mohorjeva družba.

THE CYCLE OF VIOLENCE: THE TRAPS OF PLAYING THE VICTIM

Tomaž Erzar & Katarina Kompan Erzar, *Ljubljana*

The term 'cycle of violence' has so far been used in the literature in two senses, first, as a vivid illustration of the recurrent pattern of intimate partner violence, and secondly, as a description of the intergenerational transmission of disorderly behavior from the parent generation to generation of children (Widom 1989). The term, however, can also be understood more broadly, pointing out that violence rarely stops and even more rarely ends, even when it does not show outwards and lies hidden only in one's interior world. In such cases violent destructiveness turns against the person himself who may become self-destructive and in extreme cases commit suicide (Widom and Maxfield 2001).

In our paper, we focus on a specific aspect of the cycle of violence known as victim playing or self-victimization which describes how people more or less consciously present themselves as victims in order to solicit sympathy from others and/or justify their own inappropriate and abusive behavior. We also describe ways to give up self-victimization through attitude and behavior change moving toward forgiveness.

1. Destructiveness and self-destructiveness

Human destructiveness is primarily directed against groups or individuals whom we perceive as a threat to our lives or lifestyle. From evolutionary perspective, this type of aggression is quite natural and understandable. Chances of survival of a group are greater if members are constantly on the lookout against external enemies and if they connect with each other, while at the same time keep distance from other groups. Destructiveness, however, can also be directed against oneself, which is much less natural and understandable. Why would someone hate herself or himself? Why would someone treat herself as bad person, unworthy of love and living? Obviously, then, an individual needs something more than just the support of his own group that comes together in times of danger, but otherwise expresses to its own people, men, women and children, the same distrust and hatred as to people outside the group. Interpersonal support, which gives meaning to life and makes it full, cannot simply be a matter of survival logic, but must radiate sympathy and kindness that go beyond group functionality. Only such support and affection make us feel loved and accepted, even when there is nothing we can contribute to the interests of the group and even when we cannot accept and love ourselves. Feeling of self-acceptance that occurs as a result of such interpersonal support is also the best counterweight to feelings of threat, fear, anger and hatred instilled in us by the outgroups (Hughes 2006).

2. Individuals and groups

The dynamics of violence takes similar forms at the level of groups and at the level of individuals (Beck 2000, 145). What we dislike and what angers us in the outgroup, will sooner or later begin to disturb us in individuals within our group, particularly in those relationships where we expect to satisfy our needs and desires, and where in this regard we depend on others. In the same way as a husband may be angry with his wife because she does not let him raise their children the way he wants, one group in a society may direct its anger to another group which in the eyes of the first group is perceived as a threat to its ambitions and vital interests. In both cases, the other party is seen as someone who should know what we need and should support us in this matter, or at least not interfere. Since this is not done, the other is perceived as unfavorable and malicious to us, which is directly reflected in our angry and hostile attitude toward him. Sooner or later this unfriendly attitude of one side will be detected by the other side which will in turn respond with shock, anger and hatred.

Usually none of the groups involved in a conflict is aware or does not want to realize that the reaction on the other side may be a very natural response to the behavior exhibited from this side, or that the behavior from one side at least contributed to the reaction on the other side. Both sides experience their anger as justified and look at the other side to spot even the smallest signs that would confirm their hostile attitude. Both sides experience themselves as victims of hostile undertakings of the other side and feel entitled to use retaliatory measures, even if they cross morally permissible boundaries and resort to insults, lies, physical violence or even murder. Justification for these acts is always looked for and found in the activities of other party, regardless of whether or not these activities are true, only half-true, or entirely fabricated.

From the described dynamics, it can be seen that part of the victim playing both in interpersonal relations and in relations between groups comes very naturally and is often used in more or less conscious manipulations. Since the victim is always right by definition, the greater the injustice suffered by the victim, the more she or he is right. Very often self-victimization is used by aggressors or abusers who not only play victim in the eyes of the public, but in their own eyes as well, although when prompted they struggle to define what exactly the victimization is about and what rights would have been denied to them. When convinced that their attack is authorized and justified, some aggressors go as far as to attack their victims in advance, in hope that through preventive, unexpected attack they obtain a decisive advantage. The same is true in intimate human relations, where for example a husband who physically abuses his wife gives himself the permission to use violence by repeatedly evoking in his own mind memories of past torts committed by her against him (Coie and Dodge 1998). He will also focus his attention on the current behavior of his wife in order to find signs of the same attitude that once has caused him suffering and then use these signs for the justification of his own misbehavior.

When people over-emphasize wrongs caused to them by others and when they use instances of more or less imaginary injustice to justify their own violent behavior and hostile attitude, we normally see through their insincere attempts at manipulating our emotions. Sometimes, however, the role of victim is assumed by people who do not act aggressively against other people and who are not perceived as violent and overtly manipulative. Neither will they portray themselves in a ridiculously self-aggrandizing manner. Usually, at some time in their past, these people were real victims of traumatic events and now in their daily lives continue to complain about their fate and blame everyone else for it.

3. Former victims as emotional abusers

Victim playing is common in children who suffered early neglect and emotional abuse (Hartley 2002). These children retain into adulthood the status of victims, despite the changed circumstances, and notwithstanding the fact that they are surrounded by people who love them and are ready to come to their aid. In most cases these people are their married partners and their own children. Insisting in the role of victim represents for these individuals a possibility to hide behind a bulwark of powerlessness, covert anger, whining and calling for help and use this shield in any situation they perceive as demanding or dangerous. When help is offered to them, they often refuse it or are unable to accept it. In themselves, they are furious and frustrated, but because they cling to anger and play helpless victim, they cannot cope with their true pain and mourn for it (Hirsch, Webb and Jeglic 2012).

Since excessively suspicious, and because they cannot honestly disclose their frustrations to their loved ones, they eventually create around them an empty space which they try to fill with superficial contacts, simulated kindness and help to other people who just as they do not need this assistance. Their hidden resentment and simulated kindness awaken in their surroundings mistrust and anger, which occasionally leads to outbreaks of aggression on one side or the other.

People who in this way become the self-defined eternal victims and martyrs have learned from their experience of abuse that relationships between people are dangerous and that it is safer to manipulate people and use them to satisfy one's hidden needs. The result of such perceptions of others and behavior towards them is that the former victims in their new families or workplace become extremely adept emotional blackmailers who exploit their loved ones for the sake of their own emotional security. Since loved ones are often emotionally dependent on these self-defined victims, they cannot defend against this abuse or protect themselves (Golomb 1992).

The role of eternal victim may also be taken by someone who was not the obvious victim of early neglect or abuse, but was in adulthood a victim of political persecution and social discrimination. On the surface, these persons' situation may seem simpler, because they do not necessarily internalize the suffering caused by political or social forces. Often, due to favorable childhood experiences, they manage to preserve a healthy core of self-confidence and sense of security that prevents them from slipping into the role of self-defined victims. Current injustice is perceived by them as a result of unfair social situation and not as a result of their fallibility or bad intentions, and thus cannot undermine their internal feeling of safety and acceptance which remains intact despite external pressures. They are able to live fully in the present and contribute to the elimination of injustice in their own society, as for example Nelson Mandela in South Africa. Such cases, however, are rather the exception than the rule. What we find more often is that current injustice awakens in these people a set of unhealed injuries and wrongs from early periods of life. As a result, current injustice and suffering deepens previous wounds to the self-esteem of these people and results in complete loss of sense of security and acceptance. People start to feel like perpetual victims who will never be able to escape wrongs in their society or start a new life elsewhere.

In order to feel secure again and be part of a safe and trusting interpersonal world, adult victims of political persecution and injustice must deal with several problems simultaneously:

a) recognize manipulative behavior and tendency to instill guilt, often used by undemocratic regimes against those who think differently;
b) deal with concrete consequences of injustice they suffered;
c) deal with the temptation to keep their pain for themselves and not talk about it;
d) deal with their anger and hatred in a way that leads to emotional awareness of deeper feelings of pain, helplessness, humiliation, aloneness and shame;
e) express these deeper feelings in a safe, intimate relationship; if no such relationship exists or is believed not to exist, existing relationships must be put to the test;
f) confront the legacy of early attachments and possible injustices in one's family of origin;
g) resist the temptation to play the victim by practicing the attitude of gratitude and forgiveness.

4. Practicing forgiveness

Due to its immediate emotional benefits, self-victimization is a very long-ranging and hardly reversible consequence of all kinds of violence and social injustice. Moreover, since deep in themselves they hold onto self-righteous resentment, anger and suspicion, self-defined victims do not hesitate to verbally or physically attack other people, by whom they feel threatened. Thus, victim mentality becomes the source of revictimization and renewed violence against others.

In the last decade research on the effects of abuse and traumatization found that former victims cannot begin to live fully in the present, until they are capable of forgiveness (Luskin 2002). Forgiveness does not mean that victims should reconcile with offenders or that they should forget the injustice done to them or should not look for compensation, but that the injustice and the associated emotions will be soothed only when victims turn to the source of good in their lives and let good things guide them to a new beginning. Instead of focusing on their pain, victims have to open themselves to safe and sincere relationships they could not recognize as such in the past, and use them as a source of support and assistance. In this way, they will learn for the first time in their lives to accept support and compassion without having to earn or beg for it, which is what they would normally do by adopting the role of self-defined victims. It is precisely this role that eventually becomes for them the only way of being in contact with other people and the only way of finding support and compassion. And it is this role that gradually turns victims into perpetrators and emotional abusers.

Practicing forgiveness implies the capacity for mourning. Since they usually cling to anger and resentment in order to avoid feeling pain and shame, victims cannot set an emotional boundary around these feelings which as a result become even more pervasive and threatening. To put an end to this emotional turmoil, victimized individuals must be fully aware of their inner pain, helplessness and sorrow and embrace the losses that come with suffering injustice. Mourning the losses and lost opportunities will gradually make room in their hearts for new experiences and new input from compassionate people.

Forgiveness, as defined above, is at the same time an intimate decision which cannot be prescribed by an authority and a process that needs outer forms and rituals to bring results. It is an attitude that gradually permeates the whole person and enables the person not only to take injustice less personally, but to discover new meaning in past wrongs.

Although the above considerations regarding victims and perpetrators rely mostly on international studies and observations, their value for studying the effects of traumatic war and post-war events in Slovenia cannot be overestimated. In the face of nondemocratic conditions and methods of intimidation used by the former socialist regime, for many years a large part of the Slovenian population experienced themselves as second-class citizens and victims of the regime, which has certainly contributed to their unwitting self-victimization, coupled with latent anger, suspicion and mistrust towards others (Erzar and Kompan Erzar 2011).

On the other hand, forced ideological black-and-white self-understanding and the absence of a genuine confrontation with the past enabled perpetrators to either stay hidden behind defense mechanisms of denial and manipulation or be condemned to silence and concealment, without the possibility of receiving compassion or understanding they would in normal circumstances be able to receive (Staub 1999). As a consequence, they were left with no means to deal honestly with their morally wrong actions. Dodging any responsibility and showing no genuine regret for the fate of victims, they also continue to fuel the process of demonizing of offenders, which is again used by victims as an argument for their continuing self-victimization (Staub 1998).

There are more than enough reasons in Slovenia to give impetus to the process of forgiveness on the side of the victims as well as on the side of the perpetrators, irrespective of their ideological affiliation. Victims who cannot cope with their anger, rage and hatred soon become perpetrators and thus extend the cycle of violence from one generation to another until this day. In the same vein, perpetrators who cannot break the loyalty to their former groups and ideologies and still hide under the umbrella of anti-social elites, help perpetuate the mass self-deception about the past and the mass denial of personal responsibility regarding post-war killings and violence. They not only contribute to black-and-white understanding of these tragic events, but foster in victims a sense of revictimization and a desire for revenge. The cycle of violence may thus again have come full circle.

References

Beck, A. T. 2000*: Prisoners of hate: The cognitive basis of anger, hostility, and violence.* New York: HarperCollins.

Coie, J. D. and Dodge, K. A. 1998: Aggression and antisocial behavior, in: W. Damon, R. M. Lerner and N. Eisenberg (eds.), *Handbook of Child Psychology. Vol. 3: Social, emotional and personality development,* pp. 779–862. 5. ed. New York: Wiley.

Erzar, T. and Kompan Erzar, K. 2011: Travma povojnih pobojev in njeno zdravljenje, v: J. Dežman (ed.), *Resnica in sočutje: prispevki k črni knjigi titoizma; poročilo 3; poročilo Komisije Vlade RS za reševanje vprašanj prikritih grobišč 2009–2011*, pp. 315–321. Ljubljana: Družina.

Golomb, E. 1992*: Trapped in the Mirror: Adult Children of Narcissists in Their Struggle for Self*, New York: Harper.

Hartley, C. 2002: The Co-occurrence of Child Maltreatment and Domestic Violence: Examining Both Neglect and Child Physical Abuse. *Child Maltreatment* 7, 4:349–358.

Hirsch, J. K., Webb, J., and Jeglic, E. 2012: Forgiveness as a moderator of the association between anger expression and suicidal behaviour. *Mental Health, Religion and Culture* 15, 3:279–300.

Hughes, D. 2006: *Building the Bonds of Attachment*, 2. ed. Lanham: Jason Aronson.

Luskin, F. 2002: *Forgive for Good: A Proven Prescription for Health and Happiness.* New York: HarperOne.

Staub, E. 1998: Breaking the Cycle of Genocidal Violence: Healing and Reconciliation, in: J. H. Harvey (ed.), *Perspectives on Loss: A Sourcebook,* pp.231–238. New York: Brunner/Mazel.

Staub, E. 1999: The roots of evil: personality, social conditions, culture and basic human needs. *Personality and Social Psychology Review* 3:179–192.

Widom, C. P. 1989: The cycle of violence. *Science*, 244:160–166.

Widom, C. P. and Maxfield, M. G. 2001: *An Update on the "Cycle of violence". Research in Brief.* Washington: U.S. Department of Justice, National Institute of Justice.

JOYFUL TRANSCENDENCE IN CHRIST. PREPARATION FOR MARTYRDOM IN SAINT THOMAS MORE'S SPIRITUAL EXPERIENCE

Marcin Godawa, *Cracow*

The topic of martyr's preparation for death refers to both further problems of genocide and suicide. Killing Christians for their faith makes a kind of contemporary genocide which is distinguished by its diversity and scale (cf. Siarko 2012, 166-183). However, Christian martyrdom from its beginning has a deep sense which surpasses horizon of earthly persecutions ('*Martyr*' 2000, 364, cf. Łydka 1998, 286-7). There is some special reason for voluntary receiving death by a martyr[1]. He rejects saving life at every price if it would be only in return for the betrayal of Christ. This leads to a question of martyr's victory by virtue of his relation to the Lord, who rules over death and shows in his Resurrection the ultimate sense of human life.

From the outer point of view, martyrdom may recall suicide on the grounds of self-decision to lose life, since in a typical situation a martyr sacrifices his life although he could save it if only he wanted to (by betrayal). But what seems to be a similarity in fact contains a fundamental difference of freedom. Martyr's sacrifice means the highest embodiment of his clear freedom while suicide may reveal a lack of a proper free will. That is why the Church conditionally accepts a suicide's Christian burial. Also a comparison between martyrdom and 'altruistic suicide' stresses their partial likeness though indeed they are differed at the point that a suicide is an active maker of his death while a martyr remains a passive one receiving his final fate only as the ultimate necessity of being faithful to God and religion (cf. Cholewa 2012, 107-127).

Anyway, giving life for the Lord provokes the next question how a man acts on the verge of death. Taking into account the characteristics of the Christian martyrdom it is very interesting and scientifically important to analyse martyr's intentional preparation for death. In the research a common structure of this work could be perceived which consists of three elements, namely: 1) regarding Christ, the Resurrected Lord, as a principle of human life 2) human's inner transcendence resulting in a new assessment of the question of life and death 3) joy as a fruit and characteristic phenomenon of Christian peace and readiness for martyrdom. This sequence is here showed by reading St. Thomas More's selected prison writings mainly: *A Godly Instruction*, *A Godly Meditation*, *A Devout Prayer* and the last letter to his daughter, Margaret, because this example makes an exceptionally persuasive argument for the thesis.

---

[1] This question could be supplemented by an issue of preparation for death in other religions (cf. Kościelniak, 2012, 67-93).

Christ as Life Principle

In the beginning it must be said that this is the Lord who stands in the center of More's experience. Following St. Paul's spirit of sacrifice the English Saint asks: 'Glorious God, give me from henceforth Thy grace with little respect to the world, so to set and fix firmly my heart upon Thee, that I may say with Thy blessed apostle st. Paul: 'Mundus mixi crucifixus est et ego mundo (Gal 6:14). Mihi vivere Christus est et mori lucrum (Philip 1:21). Cupio dissolvi et esse cum Christo' (Philip 1:23) (More, *A Devout Prayer*). More intentionally repeats Paul's confession that 'life is Christ, and death is gain' applying it to himself as his own personal belief. He also regards the Lord as fundamental principle of his life so that he does not want to live without Jesus. Furthermore, he evokes Paul's dilemma (Philip 1:23) with the same desire to leave the world for Christ. Likewise this tendency is made by God's grace, here spoken directly. God is able and ready to transform a human heart in order to overcome the world and choose the only way to achieve eternal life.

Like Paul, Thomas continues expressing his faith in a meditation on Christ's Paschal deed and in *A Devout Prayer* he leaves several traces of that. He strongly wants to refer his sufferings to the Lord's: 'Good Lord, give me the grace, in all my fear and agony, to have recourse to that great fear and wonderful agony that Thou, my sweet Saviour, hadst at the Mount Olivet before Thy most bitter passion, and in the meditation thereof to conceive ghostly comfort and consolation profitable for my soul' (More, *A Devout Prayer*). This sentence could be named a program of meditation during tribulation. Here two subjects appear: a man and Christ with their own experiences. A man's fear and agony are connected to Christ's Passion by means of grace in the sense of spiritual (and sacramental) communion. The prisoner perceives himself as not separated but diverted towards God. This parallel is realized by the motive of watch before death as at the Mount Olivet as in Tower. Meditation in this state leads to 'ghostly comfort and consolation', that is with gifts which a martyr needs so much and which opens a perspective of joy. A way of description should also be noticed. The figure of Jesus bears very often an adjective 'sweet' whereas His passion is 'bitter'. This contrast evokes the Son's of God self-humiliation (*kenosis*), considered by Paul (Philip 2:5-11). The epithet 'sweet Saviour' addresses to a great Christian tradition of using a word 'sweet' towards Jesus as well as to human spiritual experience (cf. Tugwell 2006, 109), especially in the late Middle Ages. Yet, on the other hand, the Passion is characterized by 'great fear and wonderful agony', which apparently interfers with 'bitterness' but in fact expresses a scale of events and maybe shows the present inward Lord's glory. It is important that a man's positive language represents his whole good experience which in connection with Thomas also asks for 'warmth' and 'delight' of his mental prayer (More, *A Devout Prayer*).

In order to supplement a picture of this union some passages are worth quoting. The relation is rendered by a motive of the Saviour's blood which washes a man: '[...] o glorious Trinity, vouchsafe, of Thy goodness to wash me with the blessed blood that issued out of Thy tender body, o sweet Saviour Christ [...]' (More, *A Devout Prayer*). A direction of flowing blood also stresses the Christ's fundamental role of being a maker of human spiritual maturity. He builds this by sacramental life, mainly reconciliation and the Eucharist, and by stirring a man with helpful gifts like longing for sacraments, 'quickness' in meditation, three theological virtues and joy. These actions should be seen along with the blood in one great stream by which a man is being transformed to reach his final aim. The martyr's way finishes not with avoiding sufferings even in purgatory or hell or with reaching heavenly goods but only with God alone: 'Give me, good Lord, a longing to be with Thee [...] nor so much for the attaining of the joys of heaven in respect of my own commodity, as even, for a very love to Thee' (More, *A Devout Prayer*). Indeed, the Holy Trinity is the principle of human life. It does not mean that More does not love himself but that his love is totally subordinated to God: 'Give me, good Lord, [...] a love to the good Lord incomparable to the love to myself and that I love nothing to Thy displeasure, but everything in an order to Thee' (More, *A Devout Prayer*). Starting from this vision of man the question of his inner transformation could now be considered wider.

Martyr's Inner Transcendence

The topic of inner transcendence could be here inaugurated by More's request including the next evocation of Paul's letter to the Philippians: 'To buy the time again, that I before have lost, to abstain from vain confabulations; to eschew light, foolish mirth; and gladness; recreations not necessary to cut off; of worldly substance, friends, liberty, life and all, to set the loss at right nought for the winning of Christ' (More, *A Godly Meditation*). This passage is built on the ground of contrast between the enumeration of goods to be thrown away and the very short presentation of obtaining Christ. The confrontation of the motive of 'the loss at right nought' with 'the winning of Christ' appealing to Philip 3:7 shows the whole perspective of crossing oneself. The contrast reveals that Christ is more precious than all the other goods, even at a biggest number. However, concentration on the Lord does not exclude the loving relation with people, friends and enemies. *A Devout Prayer* finishes with prayers for both groups. Also More's last letter consists of short instructions addressed to his close relatives whom he loves in the name of the Lord. The warmth of words written a day before his execution proves that the prisoner remained a genuine humanist. This catalogue of last issues could be juxtaposed with the numerous catalogues of earthly values which More has already overcome and left. The idea of inner transcendence is then depicted by diverse types of contrast, i.e. a catalogue (*enumeratio*) versus one element or a catalogue versus the other collection.

Despite being a prisoner a man engages his freedom in making a principal choice, that is to leave everything for Christ, to regard each good as 'the loss' in order to gain the union with the Saviour. The free action consists not only of this decision but also of all meditations, prayers and especially of accepting the day of execution with which a court appointment of that day does not interfere. In his last letter Thomas writes: 'I should be sorry if it were to be any longer than to-morrow: for it is St. Thomas even, and the utas [vigil] of St. Peter; and therefore to-morrow long I to go to God; it were a day very meet and convenient for me' (*Thomas More's last letter*). A cooperation of human free will and reason with grace brings about formulating a new interpretation of the situation. The outer death sentence is approved by a man so that he perceives the last day from a religious point of view and therefore he desires that day as a 'convenient' one.

This attitude shows that a privileged area of inner transcendence signifies a change of mind. Also Paul gives advice: 'Be transformed by the renewal of your mind' (Rom 12:2, New American Bible). Thomas More intensively collaborates with grace to improve and keep his thinking strong. A work of meditation produces a new attitude towards worldly goods, himself and the other people whereof an epitome is a new logic. Thanks to it the martyr regards his situation as meaningful. Like Paul, More sees unceasingly the principle of his life, i.e. Christ, that determines his relation to the rest of reality. The general scheme of this action presents itself as following: to attain Jesus as much as possible so as to set oneself free from the world and also from one's own weaknesses and to distribute spiritual peace among others. Because of building on the transcendent grounds this mental state is coherent and reasonable though an expression of that can surprise. In *A Godly Meditation* the author considers a biblical scene with Joseph claiming that his brothers could have never done so much good for him with their love and favour as they did with their malice and hatred (More, *A Godly Meditation*). It reproduces Paul's conclusion that even people's wrong motivation ultimately serves for proclaiming Christ. But the brilliant example of this logic sounds in *A Godly Instruction* where More undertakes a problem of love of enemies. His extraordinarily bright reason generates a perceptive analysis dividing the problem into two ways which lead to one conclusion - not to hate but love them. These two ways are two possible alternative situations and contemporaneously two arguments. Here an opponent can be saved, if he converts himself to God, or damned, if he remains sinful. *Tertium non datur*. Thomas develops the first situation as follows: 'If he be saved, he shall not fail, if I be saved too, as I trust to be, to love me very heartily, and I shall then love him likewise. And why, then, should I now hate one, who shall hereafter love me for evermore? And why should I now be an enemy to him, with whom I shall, in time coming, be coupled in eternal friendship?' (More, *A Godly Instruction*). Accordingly, he should also be treated with love: 'If he shall continue nought and be lost, that is so terrible and eternal a sorrow to him, that I should think myself a cruel wretch, if I did not now rather pity his pain, than malign his person' (More, *A Godly Instruction*). One appeal to the eschatological truth about man supplies two reasons for loving others in every case so that supernatural love makes the only logical solution. Likewise Thomas uses an example of Stephen and Saul-Paul who despite their different roles in the past are friends in heaven for ever. (*The Life of Sire Thomas More*, 54-55) Heavenly glory determines the ultimate interpretation of earthly life like in an example of a mother who does not longer remember her pain of giving birth to a child (J 16:21).

Joy as Fruit of Preparation

The inner transcendence turning a man from the world to Christ expresses then itself in mental brightness and leads logically to strong joy. This phenomenon could be very often observed in More's prayers and life. Joy is a grace for which the prisoner asks frequently: 'Gladly to be thinking of God; piteously to call for His help; to lean onto the comfort of God' (More, *A Godly Meditation*). The joy is experienced along with and through sufferings: 'gladly to bear my purgatory here; to be joyful of tribulations; to walk the narrow way that leadeth to life' (More, *A Godly Meditation*, cf. Mt 7:14). The perspective of eternal life is a source of gladness wherefore sorrow is accepted as a way leading to heaven, according to the Gospel. However, More's reason and will are directed solely to this divine joy excluding categorically any earthly enjoyment so that he begs for a deliverance from worldly sadness and joy as well as for being gifted with both sadness and joy but only as coming from the Lord. The request is parallelly constructed: 'O glorious God, all sinful fear, all sinful sorrow and pensiveness, all sinful hope, all sinful mirth and gladness take from me. And on the other side, concerning such fear, such sorrow, such heaviness, such comfort, consolations and gladness as shall be profitable for my soul: Fac mecum secundum magnam bonitatem tuam Domine' (More, *A Devout Prayer,* cf. Ps 118:29, 145:7-8). That also proves the principal role of Jesus who manages human's life. Such free dependence on the Lord St. Ignatius Loyola, thirteen years younger than More, describes as indifference (*indifferentia*): 'For this it is necessary to make ourselves indifferent to all created things in all that is allowed to the choice of our free will and is not prohibited to it; so that, on our part we want not health rather than sickness, riches rather than poverty, honor rather than dishonor, long rather than short life, and so in all the rest; desiring and choosing only what is most conducive for us to the end for which we are created' (*The Spiritual Exercises of St. Ignatius of Loyola*, 14).

A special sign of spiritual joy is gentleness. More's whole attitude along with his speech before the court proves to what extend he possesses that virtue. The prisoner does not address any complaints to the king but on the contrary he enlists all the favors received from His Majesty (*The Life of Sir Thomas More*, 51-52), expresses his gratitude for his consent to More's daughter's presence at the burial and also assures the king of his prayers for him (*The Life of Sir Thomas More*, 57). Thomas More's art of attaining spiritual greatness and kindness reveals itself in his last actions on the day of execution. According to Roper's report: 'going up the scaffold, which was so week that it was ready to fall, he [More] said merrily to Master Lieutenant, “I pray you, Master Lieutenant, see me safe up, and for my coming down let me shift for myself”. Next he turned to the executioner speaking 'with a cheerful countenance': 'Pluck up thy spirits, man, and be not afraid to do thine office; my neck is very short, take heed therefore thou strike not awry, for saving of thine honesty' (*The Life of Sir Thomas More*, 58). Perceived as furthest from terror of death, these merry sayings show by amplification the greatness of the martyr's victory. Even if then convicts made their executions a kind of spectacle (*a hanging match*; Lipoński, 2003, 343-346), More made it in a very Christian way as a saint and a fully developed man.

Conclusion

On the grounds of Thomas More’s prison writings the experience of Christian martyrdom can be displayed by the scheme: 1) Christ as a principle of overcoming death – 2) the inner transcendence of the way of life hitherto – 3) joy as fruit. By using this chain a nature of spiritual life which connects both objective and subjective dimensions is shown. The Lord as the Creator and the resurrected Saviour is alone an objective foundation for human life after death. To this 'pure objectiveness' a martyr is getting subordinated by the inner transcendence in order to express his final similarity to Christ. In this process a man’s own subjectivity is being adapted for the objective rule of life in sense that a man takes the consequences of choosing Jesus. However, the human personality does not disappear but it is totally integrated with Christ's life. A peculiar sign of that is joy which proves how much subjective spiritual life reflects the presence of divine objectiveness. According to the aim of theology of spirituality, which is a description of spiritual experience, the scheme showed here may serve as a point of references in further research as well as in forming one's personal life not only facing a direct perspective of death but also in ‘everyday little martyrdom' where love still turns out to be stronger than sinful death.

References

‘*Martyr*’ in: E. A. Livingstone (ed.), 2000: *The Concise Dictionary of the Christian Church*, Oxford University Press, p. 364.

Cholewa, M. 2012: *Męczeństwo formą samobójstwa?,* in: S. Drzyżdżyk (ed.), *Męczeństwo: przeszłość - teraźniejszość - przyszłość*, Kraków: Wydawnictwo <<scriptum>>, pp. 107-27.

Kościelniak, K. 2012: *Męczeństwo - chrześcijańska wyłączność?*, in: S. Drzyżdżyk (ed.), *Męczeństwo: przeszłość - teraźniejszość - przyszłość*, Kraków: Wydawnictwo <<scriptum>>, pp. 67-93.

Lipoński, W. 2003: *Dzieje kultury brytyjskiej*, Warszawa: Wydawnictwo Naukowe PWN.

Łydka, W. 1998: '*Męczeństwo*' in: A. Zuberbier (ed.), *Słownik Teologiczny*, Katowice: Księgarnia Św. Jacka, p. 286-7.

More T., *A Devout Prayer*, http://www.luminarium.org/renlit/morebio.htm (accessed September 23, 2013) (following Bridgett, T. E. 1892: *The Wisdom and Wit of Blessed Thomas More*, London: Burns and Oates, Ltd., 1892, 94-7).

More T., *A Godly Instruction*, http://www.luminarium.org/renlit/morebio.htm (accessed September 09, 2013) (following Walter, W. J. 1840: *Sir Thomas More: His Life and Times* London: Charles Dolman, 314-5).

More T., *A Godly Meditation*, http://www.luminarium.org/renlit/morebio.htm (accessed September 23, 2013) (following Bridgett, T. E. 1892: *The Wisdom and Wit of Blessed Thomas More*, London: Burns and Oates, Ltd., 92-4).

New American Bible, http://www.usccb.org/bible/ (accessed November 25, 2013).

Siarko, V. 2012: *Jana Pawła II teologia męczeństwa w kontekście działalności beatyfikacyjno-kanonizacyjnej męczenników*, in: S. Drzyżdżyk (ed.), *Męczeństwo: przeszłość - teraźniejszość - przyszłość*, Kraków: Wydawnictwo <<scriptum>>, pp. 166-83.

The Life of Sir Thomas More c. 1556 by William Roper, http://www.thomasmorestudies.org/docs/Roper.pdf (accessed September 23, 2013).

The Spiritual Exercises of St. Ignatius of Loyola, http://www.ccel.org/ccel/ignatius/exercises.html (accessed November 22, 2013).

Thomas More's last letter, http://www.luminarium.org/renlit/morebio.htm (accessed September 23, 2013) (following Walter, W. J. 1840: *Sir Thomas More: His Life and Times*, London: Charles Dolman, 345-7).

Tugwell, S. 2006: *Drogi niedoskonałości*, trans. A. Gomola, Poznań: W drodze.

SUICIDAL IDEATION IN RELATIONSHIPS PRIOR TO MARRIAGE AND ITS IMPACT ON DECISIONS WHETHER A MARRIAGE BETWEEN SUCH COUPLES CAN BE ANNULLED

Stanislav Slatinek, *Ljubljana*

Human life is most usually regarded as a precious possession, a divine gift, a sacred obligation, or a lucky and beautiful source of joy. Yet a small number of us humans seem to hold a very different attitude, trying to end our own lives. Many theories have been put forward to account for suicide (Milton 2009, 75-77).

Emotional distress has long been recognized as an important contributing factor in suicides. For example, suppose a man has a serious argument with his girlfriend. He would like to be married, but, at that particular time, his girlfriend does not agree. According to the hopelessness theory, if the man believes that the dispute could damage their relationship and will eventually lead to his girlfriend breaking up with him, he is likely to become hopeless and suicidal (Meckle 2004, 71). The act of attempting suicide by one of the parties can result in pressure being put on the other person in the relationship; specifically, pressure from friends and/or family (Juhant 2012, 16-17) to continue the relationship and perhaps even encouragement for the couple to eventually marry. Most usually this pressure is put on the person in the relationship who does not have suicidal ideation. For our analysis today I have looked at the connection between this pressure and how it influenced decisions made by the Romanae Rotae relating to the annulment of marriages. The fact that one member of the couple attempted to take their own life prior to getting married should alert us to the possibility that future negative events can result in further negative consequences or outcomes during the marriage. In this situation we must remind ourselves of the obligations which all who prepare those for marriage have.

A number of Rotae Romanae tribunal cases (from 1990 to 2000), sufficiently significant for this paper, have demonstrated a powerful link between displays of hopelessness on one side and attempts at suicide on the other. This connection has been evident both during the relationships prior to getting married and in the marriages. Studies have shown that hopelessness is a better indicator of suicidal ideation among those who attempted to take their own lives than depression (Joiner 2007). I hope, in a later section, to give further clarification of the link between hopelessness and suicide. Moreover, I should point out that, after reviewing the cases of the Rotae Romanae tribunal over a 10-year period (from 1990 to 2000) it is certainly possible to hypothesize that hopelessness can result in eventual suicide of spouses with suicidal ideation.

The hopelessness theory of suicidality

The every-day term "hopelessness" captures the two core elements of this "hypothesized proximal sufficient cause", firstly, negative expectations that the person has about the occurrence of highly valued outcomes and, secondly, the perceived inability of this individual to change these unfavourable outcomes. In hopelessness theory, there are three necessary components which need to be simultaneously present to provoke a suicide attempt. These three components are; negative life events, negative cognitive style (a pessimistic view of the individual's future) and finally hopelessness (Gunnell 2005, 35-40). Studies have demonstrated that in the vast majority of cases where these are present, suicide results. The figure 1 below shows the interlinked nature of these three necessary and equivalent components.

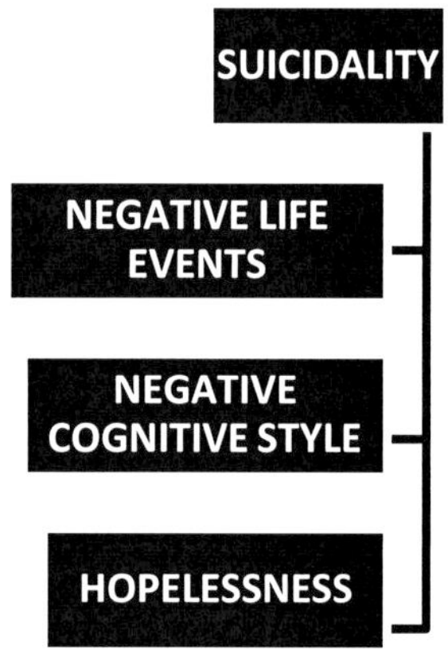

Figure 1: The hopelessness theory of suicidality

How does a person become hopeless? As can be seen in Figure 1, the hypothesized causative chain begins with the occurrence of an important event in a person's life which is perceived as negative. In hopelessness theory, negative events serve as "occasion setters" that is, circumstances which, if they arise, the people concerned become hopeless. For this study it should be stressed that the occasion setting negative events we are examining, occur in the period before marriage. In brief, relatively generalized hopelessness and, in turn, suicidality are likely to develop when negative life events are viewed as being so important for the individual that they have a very great impact on the person's entire future life. Moreover, when the fiancé experiences these negative phenomena, he/she views marriage with even greater importance (41-46). Therefore, in this situation, if one fiancé does not wish to proceed with the marriage, then the other partner feels completely alone in the world and feels that they have lost everything that he/she loves.

It is important to recognize that in many Rotae Romanae cases refusal to marry a particular person is a negative event for the other person in the relationship and when analysed by the person who wishes to proceed with the marriage, leads to negative cognitive style (Ragni 1994, 725). That is, the initial emotional upset becomes ingrained in their mind. It is perhaps important to state that negative life events do not lead to negative cognitive style and then hopelessness in all cases; many individuals deal with such disappointments in other ways. It should also be repeated here that the Rotae Romanae tribunal cases which have been used for this study are those where the individuals concerned did marry. The Rotae Romanae uses the phrase "cognitive vulnerability" to refer to this depressive cognitive style which emerges after the negative event (726-729). This cognitive analysis of the negative event creates vulnerability in the individual and is a further aspect of hopelessness theory.

An attempt at suicide is perhaps the most paradoxical of behaviours. Edwin Shneidman, an American psychiatrist gives a clear description of attempted suicide, where he sees an attempt at suicide as a perceived "loss of love and intimacy, a loss of creativity and hope" (Shneidman 1996, 84). He goes on to define attempted suicide as a "multi-dimensional malaise" which is viewed as the best solution to the predicament in which the frustrated person who is in a relationship and wants to marry finds himself/herself (85).

Self-destructive behaviours

When looking at figure 1 it showed us that, where negative life events, negative cognitive style and hopelessness exist in the period before marriage, they can lead to attempts at suicide in that period. We need now to look at the space that exists in the figure between these three components and suicidality. This is the area occupied by self-destructive behaviour; where the partner who wishes to proceed with the relationship and the plan to marry engages in self-harming actions in situations where they perceive that the relationship may end and the couple not marry. This behaviour can often be used as a way of putting pressure to marry on the other person in the relationship.

When presenting an analysis of cases which are appropriate for this study the Rotae Romanae made a distinction between those cases which involved attempted suicide on the one hand and those where there was self-destructive behaviour on the other.

To summarize the information which is included in figure 1 we can now see that the hopelessness theory can be useful in understanding the psychosocial processes which can lead to actions and ideas ranging from self-destructive behaviour, including suicidal ideation, to suicidality.

While attempted suicide is not as common as self-destructive behaviour by those experiencing difficulties in relationships (i.e. negative life events, negative cognitive style) the Rotae Romanae does acknowledge the worrying prevalence of attempted suicide in the wider population. Their reports suggest that the hopelessness theory may be especially useful to understand the situations which give rise to self-destructive behaviour and/or suicidality.

We typically think of attempted suicide (the most extreme form of self-destructive behaviour) as a sudden dramatic action where the person tries to end his/her own life. However, and more particularly, in the cases connected with marriage which we are looking at, attempted suicide is not a sudden self-destructive action but rather an undertaking which results from living without joy for a long period during the time of the relationship before marriage. It occurs when there are difficulties between the partners.

In this regard, a number of researchers, for example Lars Mehlum and colleagues have examined the relationship between attributional vulnerability and how it impacts on the behaviour of the individual with regard to personal care and health matters (Mehlum 2005, 122-130). They go on to suggest that suicidal behaviour among fiancés could be considered as a general term encompassing parasuicide and suicidal ideation. In a development of the idea of attributional vulnerability, several Rotae Romanae tribunal examples have used the term "parasuicide" to refer to all terms attributed to self-harming behaviour such as attempted suicide, suicidal gesture or self-mutilation (Funghini 1994, 17; Faltin 1995, 618). As we will see, the mood and/or outlook of the person in the relationship before marriage has an influence on their actions both before and after marriage; this can manifest itself in a number of ways and can lead to different behaviour.

Ingeborg Rossow suggested that suicidal behavior is an effort to stop the unbearable flow of negative effects. (Rossow 2005, 165-210) This links it to the negative life events which we saw in figure 1. Suicidal behaviour could be considered entirely a response to the problem of negative mood and is an attempt to regulate it. For example, a series of Rotae Romanae tribunal cases which looked at the relationships of couples before marriage outline what those who attempted suicide think about.

Very often there were conversations such as: "Non voglio piú saperne di te, me ne vado, addio. Se tu mi abbandonassi e non mi avessi sposata, io mi sarei tolta la vita!" (Palestro 1994, 170) An approximate translation: "I no longer want to be with you. I'm leaving. If you leave me and won't marry me, I will take my own life!"

Hopelessness is well-recognized as a powerful proximal cause of suicidal behaviour. Because the individual has a strong belief that he/she is powerless to regulate negative moods, they are confronted with only two terrible choices: a lifetime of unending distress or an attempt to end their lives.

Suicidal behaviour can also be linked to the problem solving abilities and coping mechanisms which the individual has. This connection between hopelessness and the person's ability to deal with disappointment can be seen in three different ways. First, the potential of the person to solve problems is disrupted by negative mood and the feeling of hopelessness. Second, a characteristic unique to that individual that makes them unable to regulate their mood and respond to negative life events. Third, attempted suicide is viewed by the suicidal individual as a solution for one's problems; one of which can be, difficult – to – regulate moods. For individuals in this predicament a self-destructive act will appear to be a help and assist them to feel better (Wrenn 1998, 75).

The person in the long term relationship (the fiancé) who develops a significant mood regulation deficit is at risk of displaying suicidal behaviour. However, suicidal behaviour will most usually be seen in the wake of what can be called a negative critical and stressful life event. There are most usually two possible results for individuals who have developed a negative mood: first, suffering some form of personality disorder or second, to become hopeless (85). For some, both can occur simultaneously or one can lead to the other.

Suicide attempts are deliberate self-harm actions that may not actually involve a desire to die, although attempts that result in serious physical harm are often motivated by fatal intent. The term "self-injurious behaviour", "self-mutilative behaviour", or "suicidal gestures" are used by some researchers to denote non-fatal self-harm acts involving motives other than a desire to die (Mehlum 2005, 125-135). The term parasuicide encompasses all types of self-harm not resulting in death. Related to this, empirical research indicates that the majority of those who have attempted suicide or engaged in self-harm do not eventually commit suicide. This paper focuses on the subgroup of suicidal individuals who attempt suicide because they only want to marry the person with whom they are in a relationship.

Suicidal behaviour in Rotae Romanae tribunal cases

In the Rotae Romanae tribunal cases, the term "attempted suicide" is used to refer to the risk factor for suicidal behaviour.

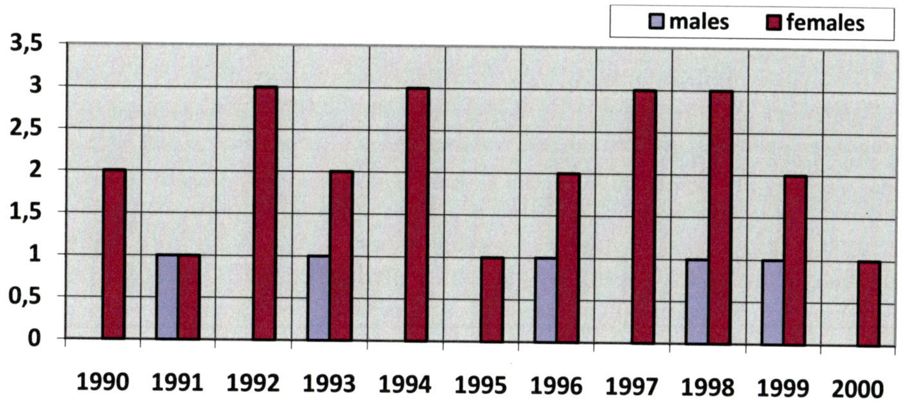

Figure 2: Analysis of granted Rotae Romanae annulment applications which were brought by spouses whose partner displayed suicidal ideation or self-harming behaviour prior to the marriage.

For the purposes of this paper, all applications in the period 1990 to 2000 to the Rotae Romanae for annulment were reviewed. From the total of 1370, it was decided that 28 were pertinent to the topic of this paper. Figure 2 provides an analysis of these 28 cases. First of all, it should be stated that requests for annulment were brought by spouses who did not have suicidal ideation or were not engaged in self-harming acts before the marriage. The information in the chart above shows that 5 males and 23 females had exhibited one or more of the following particular behaviours when confronted with an event that they considered negative before the marriage: weeping, stealing, running away, shouting, screaming, shrieking and so on (Ragni 1994, 724-726). It can quickly be seen that there were a far higher number of female suicide attempters. It should be noted that the figures in this particular context (relationships and marriage) are a complete reversal of the actions of males and females with regard to suicidal behaviour in general. For example, an analysis of figures from some European countries reveals that men are generally twice to three times more likely than women to commit suicide.

The divergent behaviour of females in long term relationships (when compared with males) is also seen when we look at the numbers of males and females in such situations who made fatal attempts to end their lives; though the proportion of women is low (4 %) no man attempted to end his own life before marriage. The Rotae Romanae cases show us that the woman usually uses self-harm behaviours (i.e. an overdose) to manipulate their fiancé (Funghini 1994, 15). A number of cases have shown that female suicidal actions are typically non-violent (16-19).

The Rotae Romanae tribunal cases reported that 26 per cent of the total number of 28 individuals (in the period 1990–2000) were under twenty-five years of age when they made suicide attempts or self-harming actions in the period before their marriage. We can also see, as was mentioned above, that the vast majority were women. Another observation indicated that some of the women in the applications made during the period were only 18 years of age when they made a suicide attempt or engaged in self-harming while in the relationship prior to marriage. A further report published in 1998 recorded that two woman who had attempted suicide before marriage were under 18 years of age; this report went on to say that: "Very young women attempted suicide for many reasons (...) many of them have serious relationship difficulties" (Wrenn 1998, 141).

Attempted suicide and self-harming in both men and women often occurs shortly after a stressful event, for example a relationship break-up. It is important to examine how important social, personal and psychological factors are for each of these people. The following emotions or perspectives can be involved in a person's decision to cease living or engage in self-harming: loneliness, social isolation, feelings of emptiness, disconnection or distance from others, experiencing a lack of control over one's life, escape from an unbearable situation, despair, depression, hopelessness, desperation, a dislike or disgust of oneself, low self-esteem or believing that a solitary life is not worth living; these are among the principle triggers leading to a suicide attempt or self-harming actions. The most frequently mentioned motives for self-harm reported by attempters are not to die, but to escape from being alone (Rossow 2005, 240-260).

A contrast can also be seen in the different reactions of men and women when confronted with sadness, rejection by the partner or disappointment. Women in these situations will display strong emotions such as weeping, fleeing from the situation etc. Whereas, on the other hand, researches have revealed that the majiority of male attempters will more usually take very dramatic/violent action. For example, while it is almost unheard of for a woman to take her own life by hanging, it is not uncommon for men to do so in situations where they are apprehensive of a negative outcome in a relationship. Many of us can perhaps also identify with the situation in our own experience where men are hindered from seeking psychiatric help because of shame, "loss of face" or loss of affection, respect etc. of their partner/fiancé. Many canon law professionals agree that people who are going through a depressive period before marriage do not have the energy or personal resources to live alone (Wrenn 1998, 33).

Though this paper deals with the Rotae Romanae cases and reported of the court in the period 1990 to 2000, the review of the 2012 tribunal cases reports that the most important symptoms and danger signs of attempted suicide are talking about or expressing a yearning for suicide. These desires to end one's life are first met by the person when they initially experience the following emotions or worries: being preocupied by the desire to marry, showing lack of interest in future plans relating to other aspects of his/her life or engaging in substance abuse (drugs, alcohol, medicines). The responses may be heightened and possibly lead to self-destructive behaviour and, in its most dramatic form, suicide (Faltin 1995, 618).

According to the findings, some of the warning signs which indicate that a young person may be suicidal are: abrupt changes in mood or behaviour, changes in eating and sleeping habits, written or verbal statements about death, saying life is not worth living or statements about feeling hopeless etc.

Conclusion

Firstly, research based on the Rotae Romanae cases from 1990 to 2000 shows that people who attempt suicide do not want to live alone; surprisingly in this context, they may also not have a great desire to die. They just want to get married. People attempt suicide to manipulate others.

Secondly, people at risk of making an attempt to end their lives are those who have a difficulty to get married or suffer from hopelessness. A small number of suicidal attempters were suffering from undiagnosed depression. Hopelessness also appears to be an integral determinant reason of a desire for death. From a study in which 28 cases were selected as appropriate for this paper, we can see that the desire for death correlated to little support or empathy from the partner or fiancé. All of these cases shared a common factor which was that each person who has attempted suicide suffered from the feeling of not being loved or from a sense of isolation.

Finally, we should consider how we can help a person who has feelings of hopelessness, is engaged in self-harming and may even have attempted suicide and may do so again. I particularly refer to those who are in a relationship but not yet married. An attempt at suicide should always be taken seriously and seen as a cry for help. Emotional support can help someone come through a suicidal crisis. Talking and listening can be a very good support; in such cases as these, counselling or therapy for the couple may be useful and may help them to communicate better and improve their ability to resolve conflict in their relationship. Medicines may also be helpful in certain cases, however, the decision to use medication should be made only after working closely with a doctor or psychiatrist. Canon lawyers, often working in the area of training priests who will be involved in the preparation of couples for marriage, have a particular responsibility to incorporate these topics in their courses. While it is extremely important to raise awareness of the issues mentioned in this paper, it is perhaps equally necessary to make those who will be involved in the area of preparing couples for marriage to be conscious both of their obligations and limitations.

References

Faltin, D. 1995: Nullitas Matrimonii. In: *Rotae Romanae Tribunal. Decisiones seu sententiae* 84, Città del Vaticano: Libreria Editrice Vaticana, pp. 617-628.

Funghini, R. 1994: Nullitas Matrimonii. In: Rotae *Romanae Tribunal. Decisiones seu sententiae* 83, Città del Vaticano: Libreria Editrice Vaticana, pp. 14-35

Gunnell, D. 2005: Time trends and geographic differences in suicide: implications for prevention. In: Hawton, K. (ed.), *Prevention and treatment of Suicidal behaviour: from science to practice,* New York: Oxford University Press, pp. 29-53.

Joiner, T. 2007: *Why People Die by Suicide*, USA: Harvard University Press.

Juhant, J. 2012. Strah in kultura strahu. In: J. Juhant, V. Strahovnik, B. Žalec (eds). *Kako iz kulture strahu? Tesnoba in upanje današnjega človeka*, Ljubljana: Teološka fakulteta, pp. 9-20.

Meckle, V. 2004: *Fatal Attachments: The Instigation to Suicide*, USA: Greenwood Press.

Mehlum, L. 2005: Traumatic stress and suicidal behaviour: an important target for treatment and prevention. In: Hawton, K. (ed), *Prevention and treatment of Suicidal behaviour: from science to practice*, New York: Oxford University Press, pp. 121-138.

Milton, C. Anne. 2009: *The Coldest Night. A Family's Experience of Suicide*, Dublin: Veritas.

Palestro, V. 1994: Nullitas Matrimonii. In: *Rotae Romanae Tribunal. Decisiones seu sententiae* 82, Città del Vaticano: Libreria Editrice Vaticana, pp. 169-175.

Ragni, H. 1994: Nullitas Matrimonii. In: *Rotae Romanae Tribunal. Decisiones seu sententiae* 81, Città del Vaticano: Libreria Editrice Vaticana, pp. 724-732.

Rossow, I. 2005: Substance use and suicidal behaviour. In: Hawton, K. (ed.), *Prevention and treatment of Suicidal behaviour: from science to practice*, New York: Oxford University Press, pp. 161-278.

Shneidman, S. Edwin. 1996: *The Suicidal Mind*, New York: Oxford University Press.

Wrenn, G. L. 1998: *The invalid Marriage*, Washington: Canon Law Society of America.

THE MEANING OF FAMILY LIFE FOR SOCIETY, DEMOGRAPHY AND WELLBEING OF CHILDREN

Tadej Strehovec, *Ljubljana*

Introduction

The wellbeing of children and the future of the society depend on the stability and quality of family life. Recent attempts in some European countries to redefine marriage and family could lead to new ethical questions, such as what exactly is the definition of family, what are the legal bases of family life, is there any difference between conventional family and new type of households like cohabitation and same-sex lifestyles, etc. Despite different political and ideological aspects regarding the redefinition of family, the historical and scientific evidence is very important for making critical analysis.

1. The historic role of the family life

Family is a group of persons united by marriage, adoption, or blood. Family members live together, and everyone has a social role: spouses, parents, children, and siblings. From the sociological point of view, family is distinguished from a household like roommates sharing a common residence. It should be also differentiated from kindred who could be divided into several households. Traditionally, the family group is based on the parent-child relationship, which may be absent from the legal marriage. The so-called nuclear family consists of two married adults, a man and a woman, who are not related by blood. Such a family is a place for their offspring. It is commonly believed that such a family is the oldest of the various types of families. In some cases, the extended nuclear family includes older parents, unmarried and married children and their offspring and elderly relatives.

Family performs different kinds of functions, like providing emotional and psychological security (through love). It is a place of procreation and is a legitimate place for sex. The nuclear family is a place for the raising and socialization of children and a place for giving care to elderly members of the family (sick, disabled). On the economic side, family provides food, shelter clothing and physical security. From the social point of view, family promotes stability and order in society. In most cultures, the most common family is male-dominated (patriarchal). During the industrialization and urbanization of Europe, extended families disappeared in big cities. After the Industrial Revolution, a greater equality between men and women developed. Caring for home and children was replaced by educational systems, the participation of women in public life and earning wages, all of which changed the social understanding of the woman's role. Having children and motherhood was no longer the main social task of women. Some couples prefer not to marry and have children; others prefer shorter relationships without legal obligation. With the legalization of divorce and the shorter duration of relationships, the number of one-parent households increased. The modern family is more consuming and socially dependent and family members work out of the home. Many family roles today have been replaced by the government-funded institutions like education, health and social systems. With the invention of artificial contraception, couples could decide when they will have children and how many children they will have.

Every culture has some form of family law, which defines the legal relationships between family members and families and society, as well. The majority of family laws contain special rules for defining marriage, the status of children and the succession of property. In general, family law defines the relation between the interests of society and individuals or families. In the nineteenth and twentieth centuries, the meaning of marriage changed due to the emancipation of women in the field of economic endeavors and property ownership. In the middle of twentieth century, the majority of European states legally defined equality between men and women. The legalization of divorce, many times via court, changed marriage and families into less stable structures. From the legal point of view, the issue of children is of great importance. Every legal system pays attention to the protection of the rights of children. Many times (especially in modern societies), the society replaces the role of parents through mandatory education. One of the facets of family law is dealing with the division of the property left by a deceased family member. Family non as a natural law based institution but as a social construct is founded on promoting responsible procreation and raising of children, caring for family members, and financial responsibility (Belsey 2001, 289-292). Such a view historically offered health, longevity, stability, security and prosperity to family members and society and culture as a whole. In the second half of twentieth century, the institution of marriage and the nuclear family diminished. With the rise of feminist and liberal ideologies, the institute of marriage is less and less attractive. Divorce, promiscuity, homosexuality, and cohabitation are in the process of "normalization" and social acceptance. Therefore, more and more people live in open relationships that are less defined, less stable and less beneficial.

2. Which are the main causes for the undermining the social role of the traditional family?

There are many different factors that could be the reason for such rapid changing of the family structures in the West like:

a. Changing perception of religious and moral message. It is well known that religion has a beneficial and important role in preserving the meaning of family life in society.

b. Universal access to the contraception, which gave to women a control and freedom to decide about time and number of children (reproductive rights). On the other side some negative consequences could be underlined like negative demographic effects; negative side effects, positive impact on prostitution, pornography, the disintegration of matrimonial and family community as well as the negative impact on marital fidelity. Analysis of the situation in the area of contraceptive use in Europe indicate a connection between increased use of contraception as well as the almost simultaneous decline in marriage and fertility, and the increase of divorce.

c. Changing of understanding of traditional social institutions like family, educational institutions, church, state and the (media) promotion of new forms of informal housing, personal freedom, emancipation of women, etc.

d. Redefinition of the concept of family. In recent decades in the West different ideas about the various forms of family lifestyles arose. Specifically the non-marital, same-sex, divorced, remarried, recombined etc. "families" are expected to be equally legitimate and "acceptable" as the conventional family of married man, woman and children. Despite the empirical fact, that only the traditional family could sustain population growth, the promotion of new non-conventional family lifestyles was done during the last 50 years. That has a negative impact on fertility and demography (Popenoe 2008). Due to unstable relationships, poverty, violence, etc. these kinds of family lifestyles are less open to procreate life as married conventional families.

e. The reduced ability of younger generations to make a formal marriage contract and preference to live in informal housing (cohabitation).

f. Finally, one of the reasons for changing family styles could be the current media pop culture (TV, Internet) where nontraditional family lifestyles are not enough promoted. It could be said the same for the role of schools which do not provide basic knowledge and information regarding marriage, family, motherhood and fatherhood.

Today new social questions arise in the field of families: What exactly is the meaning of family? Is marriage founded in human nature defined during a long human history or it is just a social construction which could be ideologically changed? Which are the main arguments to support the redefinition of marriage or to keep it in conventional or traditional way? Why less people would like to marry, and what is the truth about cohabitation and nuclear family? In the pluralistic modern society, there are many beliefs and traditions regarding the family styles.

3. Why the nuclear family still matters? The evidence from social and biological sciences

Today it is difficult to justify the conventional sense of marriage and family only at the level of philosophical and anthropological discourse. It is important to use the scientific language of social sciences, which in modern society could justify the benefits of marriage and family life. The researches focus on different aspects of marriage and cohabitation: family, economics, education, physical health and longevity, mental health, emotional well-being and crime, and domestic violence. Researches demonstrate that family structure matters for children and adults. The family structure that helps children the most, is a family headed by two biological parents in a low-conflict marriage (Anderson Moore 2002, 5). Marriage increases the likelihood that fathers have good relationships with their children. Fathers and mothers are affected by the absence of the marriage. Single mothers report more conflicts with children than do married mothers. Children from intact families have more close relations with their parents than children from divorced families (Amato and Booth 1997). In United States 30 percent of young adults had poor relations with their divorced mothers compared to 16% of children whose parents stayed married. The children relationships with their fathers are even at greater risk (Zill et al. 1993). In general, the children of divorced or never married parents have less stable relationship with fathers than do children from married families (Seltzer and Bianchi 1988). It is interesting that divorce has impact that is more negative on relationship between children and parents than remaining in an unhappy marriage. Cohabitating couples usually resemble more to the single than married couples in terms of emotional well-being, physical and mental health (Pienta, Hayward, in Jenkins 2000). Children living in married families are more likely to score higher in reading comprehension as fourth graders (Marquardt 2005, 27). Such children are about 30 percent less likely to miss school. The effect of family structure on children's educational performance could be more evident in high school graduation rates. Children living in intact, married households are about twice as likely to graduate from high school, compared to children reared in single-parent families. One study found that 37 percent of children born outside of marriage and 31 percent of children with divorced parents dropped out of high school, compared to 13 percent of children from intact families headed by a married mother and father (McLanahan in Sandefur 1994, 162). Marriage influences the emotional health of children. Children from married families are less likely to suffer from depression, anxiety, alcohol and drug abuse, and thoughts of suicide compared to children from divorced homes (Marquardt 2005, 169-182). The same results could be find from the study of Swedish boys and girls in two-parent homes which were about 50 percent less likely to suffer from suicide attempts, alcohol and drug abuse, and serious psychiatric illnesses compared to children reared in single-parent homes (Ringback Weitoft 2003, 291). Family structure influences the sexual development of girls. Only 5 percent of girls who grew up in an intact family got pregnant as teenagers, compared to 10 percent of girls whose fathers left after they turned six, and 35 percent of girls whose fathers left when they were preschoolers (Ellis et al. 2003, 818-820). The influence of family structure on boys is more significant. One-study proofs that boys reared in single parent or step-families were more than twice as likely to end up in prison, compared to boys reared in an intact family (Harper in McLanahan 2004, 390-395). Marriage has also significant benefits for men and women. Very often, the financial advantages are mentioned. Married man earns between 10 and 40 percent more money than cohabitating or single man with similar education (Marquardt 2005, 112). Usually married couples spend money in more responsible way than others do. Married adults have longer lives, less illness, less level of depression and less alcoholism and drug addiction. Many sociological studies show that cohabitating couples in comparing with married couples more often challenge with divorce (Adkins 2008); with more conflicts (Anderson Moore 2002), more risk for poverty (McLanahan 2000, 704), greater rates of suicide and mental illnesses (Cutler, Glaeser, in Norberg 2001, 64; Hetherington in Kelly 2002;), less physical health (Lundberg 1993, 1050), lower education (Jaynes 2000, 90-92), antisocial behavior (Harper in McLanahan 2004, 390-392), unwanted pregnancy (Hetherington in Kelly 2002, 87), shorter lifespan (Schwartz 1995, 1240), less stable relationships with parents (Gallagher 2006), more risk of contracting sexually transmitted diseases and infidelity in partner relationships (The Witherspoon Institute 2008, 14). Therefore, the claims that all kinds of family life are of the same quality are unfounded and are not supported by scientific researches.

Conclusion

Family is an important structure for the future of any society. The wellbeing of children and the society is dependent on the stability of families. Historically, the legal structure of the family was stable and well defined. In recent decades, however, new ideas and ideologies have influenced the legal definition of family life and marriage. The discussion about the role of family in the past and in the future is very important. Changing this fragile structure could have different kinds of long-term negative consequences that might prove very difficult to eliminate. Therefore, further research in the field of anthropology and family life will be welcome.

References

Adkins, Kate S. 2008. *Implications of violent and controlling unions for mother's menthal health leaving*. Columbus: The Ohio State University.

Amato, Paul R., and Alan Booth. 1997. *A generation at risk: growing up in an era of family upheaval.* Cambridge, Mass; London: Harvard University Press.

Belsey, Catherine. 2001. Denaturalizing the family. *European Journal of Cultural Studies* 4 (3): 289-303.

Cutler, David M., Edward Glaeser & Karen Norberg. 2001. *Explaining the Rise in Youth Suicide:* Working paper no. 1917. National Bureau of Economic Research.

Ellis Bruce et al. 2003. Does Father Absence Place Daughters at Special Risk for Early Sexual Activity and Teenage Pregnancy? *Child Development* 74: 801-821.

Gallagher, Maggie. 2006. If Marriage is Natural, Why is Defending it so Hard? Taking up the Challenge to Marriage in the Pews and the Public Square. *Ave Maria Law Review* 4(2):409-433.

Harper, Cynthia, and Sara McLanahan. 2004. Father Absence and Youth Incarceration. *Journal of Research on Adolescence* 14 (3): 369-397.

Hetherington, E. Mavis, and John Kelly. 2002. *For Better or for Worse: Divorce Reconsidered.* New York: W.W. Norton.

Jaynes, William H. 2000. The Effects of Several of the Most Common Family Structures on the Academic Achievment of Eight Graders. Marriage & Family Review 73 (1-2): 73-97.

Lundberg, O. 1993. The impact of childhood living conditions on illness and mortality in adulthood. *Social science & medicine* 36:1047-52.

Marquardt Elizabeth. 2005. *Between Two Worlds: The Inner Lives of Children of Divorce.* New York: Crown.

———. 2005. *Family Structure and Children's Educational Outcomes.* New York: Institute for American Values.

McLanahan, Sara, and Gary D. Sandefur. 1994. *Growing up with a single parent: what hurts, what helps.* Cambridge, Mass.: Harvard University Press.

McLanahan, Sara. 2000. Family, State and Child Wellbeing. *Annual Review of Sociology* 26: 703-706.

Moore, Kristin et al. 2002. Marriage from a Child's Perspective: How Does Family Structure Affect Children, and What Can We Do about It? *Child Trends Research Brief.*Http://www.childtrends.org/wp-content/uploads/2002/06/MarriageRB602.pdf

Pienta, Amy Mehraban, Mark D. Hayward, and Kristi Rahrig Jenkins. 2000. Health Consequences of Marriage for the Retirement Years. *Journal of Family Issues* 21 (5): 559-586.

Popenoe, David. 2008. *Cohabitation, Marriage and child wellbeing. A Cross-National Perspective.* Piscataway: The National Marriage Project.

Ringback Weitoft Gunilla, Anders Hjern, Bengt Haglund, and Mans Rosen. 2003. Mortality, Severe Morbidity, and Injury in Children Living with Single Parents in Sweden: A Population-Based Study. *The Lancet* 361: 289-295.

Schwartz, Joseph E. et al. 1995. Sociodemographic and Psychosocial Factors in Childhood as Predictors of Adult Mortality. *American Journal of Public Health* 85: 1237-1245.

Seltzer J.A. and S.M. Bianchi. 1988. Children's Contact with Absent Parents. *Journal of Marriage and the Family* 50: 663-677.

The Witherspoon Institute. 2008. *Marriage and the Public Good: Ten Principles.* Princeton, New Jersey: The Witherspoon Institute.

Zill Nicholas et al. 1993. Long-Term Effects of Parental Divorce on Parent-Child Relationships, Adjustment, and Achievement in Young Adulthood. *Journal of Family Psychology* 7 (1): 91-103.

ABSTRACTS

Janez Juhant
Suicide and Genocide in the Context of Modernity

There is exposed connectedness of genocide and suicide with the sideways - mostly depersonalisation of man in the society of modernity. Interpersonal relations are the source of human stability which assures a person the protection against total obedience to the other or to despair over himself. This leads man to depression and suicide, or he becomes as a number and is completely at the disposal of authoritarian and totalitarian regimes. The modern age has led to the situation when human endeavours of generations were destroyed in a moment and man was reduced to helpless cattle (Grossman 1995). How to come to a dialogical-empathic society which overcomes this catchiness of the modernity? Permanent dialogue among persons opens them for transcending all that and for making a new world of cooperation. Christianity and other religions support the paths toward empathic humanity (to overcome the suicidal or genocidal obsession).

Key words: Modernity, genocide, suicide, totalitarianism, isolation, dialogue, faith.

Bojan Žalec
Factors and Indicators of Genocide

Factors and indicators of genocide are only one part (already itself very complex) of the complete and complex picture of genocide. Yet this part is in a certain sense most central since without it no other part of the picture of genocide (its conceptual analysis and definition, its discerning from the similar phenomena (mass murders, crime against humanity etc.), strategies to prevent or to decrease the chances of it, coping with its consequences etc.) can be provided in a grounded, verified and efficient way. The essay offers a synthetic survey of factors and indicators of genocide as they are revealed by many different scientific disciplines and combination of them (multidisciplinary approach): cultural anthropology, history, (social) psychology, science of politics etc. Its aim is to contribute - or make it easier - to more integral picture and understanding of genocide.

Key words: Factors and indicators of genocide, sources of information about genocide, political aspects of genocide, anthropological and psychological aspects of genocide, essentialization and genocide.

Branko Klun
Despair and Suicide. A Kierkegaardian Reflection

With the aid of Kierkegaard and his anthropological presuppositions, the question of suicide can be restated in a completely different way. A "killing of oneself" (sui-cidium) requires reflection about what the "self" actually is. At the beginning of his work *Sickness unto Death* Kierkegaard offers an anthropological analysis of the self, which is interpreted as a mode of life which must be attained by the individual, a task which is by no means easy. And, it is precisely because man does not attain this authentic self that he finds himself in a state of despair. In the Kierkegaardian perspective the problem of suicide is shifted from the physical aspect of existing to the loss of that life; a life in which the individual is not himself, and in which he has "lost" his true self, despite still being physically alive.

Key words: Despair, suicide, Kierkegaard, self, authenticity.

Robert Petkovšek
Suicide and Genocide in the Light of Girard's Mimetic Theory

René Girard derives his mimetic theory from the axiom that man owes his origin and development to mimetic desire, which is much stronger in man than in animals. Mimetic desire frees humans from natural mechanisms to create culture. However, mimetic desire not only makes humans free but also subordinates them to mimetic mechanism that leads to mimetic crisis and sacrificial murder. Mimetic desire and the freedom deriving from it are thus agents of murder. In pre-Christic, archaic culture mimetic desire was ritually controlled. However, in modern society, which is based on freedom acquired by Christ on the cross, sacrificial mechanism is no longer ritually controlled. Freedom itself tends to be radical. Within this new framework mimetic desire creates mimetic violence that is expressed in extreme forms, such as genocide and suicide, and may reach apocalyptic proportions. The alternative to such violence is the obedience to the will of God the Father that Christ showed on the cross and was thus able to renounce mimetic desire and to step out of mimetic circle.

Key words: Suicide, genocide, mimetic theory, mimetic desire, René Girard, Dostoevsky, Gelassenheit.

Vojko Strahovnik
On the Concept of Genocide from the Point of View of Groups and Harm

The article deals with the definition of genocide, especially with the aspect of group and harm done with it to members of the group, to the group and to humanity as a whole. It highlights two distinct conceptions of harm associated with the crime of genocide. The first conception bases harm on the instrumental value of a group and sees it as a loss of status that affects the individual as a member of the group. The second conception is based on the presupposition of the intrinsic value of a group and consequently harm in the event of genocide is understood as a loss of that value to humankind. The paper concludes with some suggestions for amendment of the definition of genocide and its proper understanding.

Key words: Genocide, crime against humanity, group, harm, value.

Jernej Letnar Černič
Beyond the Legal Definition of Genocide

Human beings can in moments of dehumanisation, pride and arrogance cause unimaginable evil. Genocide represents the most radical and irrational evil, which many experts have often described as a “crime of crimes”. The legal definition of genocide therefore includes at least five elements: genocidal specific intent, genocidal offense, attack the victims because of their membership in a protected group, genocidal action should be part of the systematic and indiscriminate attacks and targeted at least partial destruction of a protected group. An effective sanctioning of such a crime plays a crucial role in purification of individual and collective consciousness. Could a legal, sociological or any other definition address all of its dimensions from real life scenarios?

Key words: Genocide, international law, protected groups, prosecution, shame, catharsis.

Béla Mester
Suicide as a Topic of the Ethical Theories in Hungarian Intellectual History under the Conditions of the Post-War Moral Crisis after the WWI

This article’s aim is to offer an analysis of an intellectual debate on the ethical and anthropological questions concerning suicide on the pages of an influential Hungarian periodical entitled *Nyugat (West)*, in the early twenties of the 20th century. This epoch is crucial concerning the topic of suicide as a theoretical problem. The high number of suicides in Hungary, the war- and post-war intellectual and moral shocks had made the cultural life sensitive for these questions. Initiator of this debate, *Jenő Posch* was a radical thinker of the late positivism. His realism was actually a consequent *physicalism;* he is a recognised predecessor of the philosophical *behaviourism*. This article offers an explanation of the plausibility of Posch’s anthropology as a frame-theory of the analysis of suicide as a problem of ethics.

Key words: Jenő Posch, philosophical anthropology, realism in philosophy, suicide, war-shock.

Gábor Kovács
"...for silent amongst rogues, I share their vice" – The Road of the Inter-war Hungarian Jewry to the Shoa from the anti-Jewish Legislation to the Deportation

The aim of this paper is to reconstruct the historical-cultural-psychological constellations of the inter-war Hungary in the context of the problem of responsibility. For the completion of this task there is used the seminal writing of István Bibó entitled '*Jewish Question in Hungary after 1944*' (1948) which has hitherto been the most comprehensive analysis including historical, cultural-religious, sociological and psychological aspects. The train of thought of his writing, in some respects runs parallel with Hannah Arendt's approach explained in the first part of '*The origins of totalitarianism.*' Both authors focus upon the problem of the relations of Jewish communities with their wider environment and they share the same hypothesis: distorted inter-communal relations involve distorted communicative situations and false experiences concerning the other party.

Key words: Shoah, Hungarian Jewry, complice, responsibility, false experience.

Tamara Griesser-Pečar
Is Destruction of a Political Group Genocide? Mass Killings in Slovenia in 1945

"Genocide" is classified as a crime under international law since December 9, 1948, when the Convention on the Prevention and Punishment of the Crime of Genocide was passed by United Nations. By definition genocide is a crime committed in time of war or peace "*with intent to destroy, in whole or in part, a national, ethnical, racial or religious group*" (Art. 2). This definition does not include the destruction of political and social groups, which is a sort of anomalism in international criminal law. They were not included because the Soviet Union and other communist countries opposed. They wanted to prevent any discussion of the victims of Soviet terror and those of other communist regimes. The question of course is, whether the fact that international law has not yet included the political and social groups into the definition of genocide, automatically means that elimination of people with similar ideas and backgrounds is less condemnable as extermination of national, ethnical, racial or religious group. The British handed over the Yugoslav refugees in Carinthia to the Yugoslav army without informing them about the rights they had according to the 1929 Geneva Convention. The British made use of a deception, as they told the prisoners that they would be transferred to the British zone in Italy (Palmanova). The contribution deals with the handovers of the Slovenian Home Guard and their civilian followers, with the fate of anticommunists and the deliberate and systematic extermination of many of them from May 1945 till

January 1946. In the present Constitution of the Republic of Slovenia however does include political as well as social groups.

Key words: Convention on the Prevention and Punishment of the Crime of Genocide, political groups, Home Guards, anticommunists, Yalta, violation of human rights, hidden graves.

Tomas Kačerauskas
Suicide in the Environment of Cultural Industry

The article deals with the issue of suicide in the contexts of creative industry and creative society. Cultural industry is inseparable from commercializing of culture and turning it into commodity, as well as from mass production and consuming of cultural products in the media environment. Thanks to the media, an individual has been purportedly liberated from his (her) existential worry, herewith from a danger of suicide. The media function as compensation of mortality, prophylaxis of suicide and promise of eternity. If a consumer of culture is the product of the media and cultural industry, we can't speak about his or her suicide: only a free and creative enough individual kills himself (herself). According to the author, suicide is the revolt of an individual against his (her) controlling from the side of society. A suicide in a creative society is both the author of an extreme self-creation, and a creator frustrated by the deficit of creation.

Key words: Suicide, media, cultural industry, creative society.

Rafal Smoczynski
The Intertwine of Integrative and Normative Potential of Religious Organizations in Constraining Suicidal Behaviour

The role of religious organizations in constraining the possibility of committing suicide triggered one of the most explored currents in sociological literature. I will use this scholarship, firstly to present recent developments of state of the arts on the efficiency of religious organizations in their potential to reduce a risk of suicide, and secondly keeping in line with the methodological approach of close critical reading of the recent revisions in the scholarship I will argue that this is the very intertwining potential of religious networking and normative teaching that offers an efficient potential of constraining suicidal behaviour. The following paper comprises 5 elements: 1) introduction demonstrating classical Durkheimian stance on the protecting influence of religion against suicide, 2) state of the arts in the literature on the interplay between religion and suicide, 3) the relevant criticism of the existing scholarship with special emphasis put on the secularist bias that implicitly underpinned significant part of the literature in the field, 4) the analysis of the differentiated approach towards religious organizations and the crucial intertwine of normative and integrative potential, 5) conclusion will be offered.

Key words: Suicide, constraining suicide, religious organizations, integrative and normative potential.

Jože Mari Osredkar
Suicide of European Civilization

The point of departure of our reflection is the claim that Europe finds itself in a crisis which is above all a crisis of the individual and his place in society. Our continent has been invaded by individualism which expresses itself, on the religious plane, as secularization and secularism. In comparing the Christian and Islamic religions, we discover that the degree of secularization is in relationship with the interpretation of Divine revelation. Islam, which does not allow any interpretation of the Qur'an, does not manifest the secularization as Christianity where anyone can interpret the Bible. Europe today accepts Christian values but refuses God and faith. Can Christian values survive without contact with their transcendental foundation? It would seem that "the refusal of God" not only equates to the dissolution of religion but also to the suicide of the Western civilization.

Key words: Europe, secularization, secularism, faith, religion.

Erika Prijatelj
Suicide and Genocide from the Perspective of Identities and Narcissism

People belong to different groups and each group can provide a person a potentially important identity. Each person is called to select his/her most important identity and to assess the relative importance of others. Different single identities contribute in shaping one's whole self-identity. It is important that due to the potential conflict between the priorities and requirements of different identities to avoid the domination of one identity over another. Such domination can nourish narcissism and trigger violence. Today we live in an era of exaggeration and of the rise of narcissism in our western culture. Narcissism is seen and accepted as normal and as a result violence toward oneself and others is on the increase. This article draws attention to the various forms of pathological narcissism and its destructive phenomenon, which can subsequently lead to metamorphic or executive suicide and genocide. The article also presents the hope of promoting healthy moral imagination and a new vision of human community.

Key words: Suicide, genocide, pathological narcissism, destructive behavior, human identities, executive identity, moral imagination.

Stanko Gerjolj
Facing Suicide and Genocide: Educational Challenges

Significant characteristics of contemporary Western civilization include existential emptiness and insecure relations in the family and wider social contexts, which leave many people in desperate situations, in which they see suicide as the only 'solution'. In this context, we recognize Moses as an encouraging biblical and teaching character, as he arises from difficult family and social circumstances, but remains in communication with God and searching for the meaning in life for others until at his very end; as an integrated personality, Moses lives a fulfilling life and, with a view into the Promised Land, dies of natural causes. Thus, the story of Moses confronts us, particularly those with responsible roles in society, with a challenge to promote enduring values and enable building relationships so as to ensure that people, despite complicated circumstances, are longing for life and discern its inner meaning, all the way to the natural end of earthly existence.

Key words: Suicide, Bible, Moses, existential vacuum, relationships, education, values, meaning.

Tomaž Erzar & Katarina Kompan Erzar
The Cycle of Violence: The Traps of Playing the Victim

Partly in response to current political atmosphere in Slovenia, we discuss different aspects of the cycle of violence in our society. We suggest that one of the most rigid problems concerns self-victimization which is defined as an act of more or less manipulative casting oneself as an eternal victim or martyr, with an aim to obtain a sympathetic response from others and justify one's own abusive behavior. We review basic notions regarding violent conflicts between individuals and groups and argue that self-victimization can only be stopped through practicing the attitude of forgiveness. Forgiveness, in the sense used in the article, is a personal process of turning to the good in life and mourning the past.

Key words: Cycle of violence, victim playing, manipulation, sincerity, forgiveness.

Marcin Godawa
Joyful Transcendence in Christ. Preparation for Martyrdom in Saint Thomas More's Spiritual Experience

This article undertakes the issue of martyr's preparation for death which, from an outer point of view, reminds us of suicide but in fact it is one's voluntary decision to sacrifice life for a greater reason. In St. Thomas More's spiritual experience written down in his prison before execution a common structure of preparation can be perceived. The profile analysed here consists of three elements, namely: 1) regarding Christ, the Resurrected Lord, as a principle rule of human life; 2) human's inner transcendence resulting in a new assessment of the question of life and death; 3) joy as a characteristic phenomenon of Christian peace and readiness for martyrdom.

Key words: Martyr, the Bible, Christ, inner transcendence, joy.

Stanislav Slatinek

Suicidal Ideation in Relationships Prior to Marriage and Its Impact on Decisions Whether a Marriage between Such Couples Can Be Annulled

Human life is most usually regarded as a precious possession, a divine gift, a sacred obligation, or a lucky and beautiful source of joy. Yet a small number of us humans seem to hold a very different attitude, trying to end our own lives. Many theories have been put forward to account for suicide. Emotional distress has long been recognized as an important contributing factor in suicides. A number of Rotae Romanae tribunal cases, have demonstrated a powerful link between displays of hopelessness on one side and attempts at suicide on the other. This connection has been evident both during the relationships and in the marriages. Studies have shown that hopelessness is a better indicator of suicidal ideation among those who attempted to take their own lives than depression. Moreover, I should point out that in the cases reviewed by the Rotae Romanae tribunal over a 10-year period (from 1990 to 2000) hopelessness resulted in eventual suicide of fiances (future spouses) with suicidal ideation. In Rotae Romanae tribunal cases hopelessnes played a central role and it is certainly possible to hypothesize that it is a cause of suicide.

Key words: Marriage, suicide, hopelessness, depression, suicidal behaviour.

Tadej Strehovec

The meaning of Family Life for Society, Demography and Wellbeing of Children

Demography is one of the most important social and economic issues in Europe. In the aging society, the question of fertility and demography, migrations and immigrations, the understanding of gender and wellbeing of children is linked to the perception and understanding of family life. What are the definitions of family, why is the conventional nuclear family many times replaced by new types of households, and why the conventional family life still matters, are some of the most important questions.

Key words: Children, cohabitation, family ethics, marriage, population.

THE AUTHORS

Janez Juhant

Prof., PhDr Theol Mag., Faculty of Theology, University of Ljubljana, Slovenia

Member of the European Academy of Sciences and Arts in Salzburg

Faculty of Theology, Poljanska 4, 1000 Ljubljana

E-mail: *janez.juhant@guest.arnes.si*

Bojan Žalec

Ph. D., Associate Prof. of Philosophy, Senior Research Fellow and Head of the Institute of Philosophy and Social Ethics

Faculty of Theology, University of Ljubljana, Slovenia

E-mail: *bojan.zalec@guest.arnes.si*

Branko Klun

Associate Prof. of Philosophy, Faculty of Theology, University of Ljubljana

E-mail: *branko.klun@teof.uni-lj.si*

Robert Petkovšek

Associate Prof. of pPhilosophy and Head of Chair for Philosophy, Faculty of Theology, University of Ljubljana

E-mail: ro*bert.petkovšek@teof.uni-lj.si*

Vojko Strahovnik

Ph. D., Faculty of Theology, University of Ljubljana

Assistant Prof. and Head of Chair for Legal Theory and Ethics & Public Policy at the Faculty of Government and European Studies in Kranj

Poljanska 4, 1000 Ljubljana

E-mail: *vojko.strahovnik@guest.arnes.si*

Jernej Letnar Černič

Assistant Prof., Faculty of State and European Studies, Kranj, Slovenia

E-mail: *jernej.letnar@googlemail.com*

Béla Mester

Ph. D., Senior Research Fellow of the Institute of Philosophy, Research Centre for Humanities, Hungarian Academy of Sciences, Budapest, Hungary; share-time associate professor of the Department of Philosophy, College of Nyíregyháza, Hungary; vice-president of the Hungarian Philosophical Society

E-mail: *mester.bela@btk.mta.hu*

Gábor Kovács

Ph. D., Senior Research Fellow of the Institute of Philosophy, Research Centre for Humanities, Hungarian Academy of Sciences, Budapest, Hungary

E-mail: *kovacsg@webmail.phil-inst.hu, gbrkvcs3@gmail.com*

Tamara Griesser-Pečar

Assistant Prof., Study Centre for National Reconciliation, Ljubljana, Slovenia

E-mail: *tamara.griesser@inode.at*

Tomas Kačerauskas

Vilnius Gediminas Technical University

Saulėtekio al. 11, LT-10223 Vilnius, Lithuania

Faculty of Creative Industries

Department of Philosophy and Political Theory

E-mail: *tomas.kacerauskas@vgtu.lt*

Rafal Smoczynski

Assistant Prof., Institute of Philosophy and Sociology of the Polish Academy of Sciences, Poland

E-mail: *rafalsmoczynski@yahoo.com*

Mari Jože Osredkar

PhD, Assistant Prof.

Faculty of Theology, University of Ljubljan, Poljanska 4, 1000 Ljubljana

E-mail: *mari.osredkar.ofm@siol.net*

Erika Prijatelj

Assistant Prof., Faculty of Theology, University of Ljubljana, Slovenia

E-mail: *erika.prijatelj@teof.uni-lj.si*

Stanko Gerjolj

Prof., Faculty of Theology, University of Ljubljana, Slovenia

E-mail: *stanko.gerjolj@teof.uni-lj.si*

Tomaž Erzar

Associate Prof., Doctorate Program in Marital and Family Therapy, Faculty of Theology, University of Ljubljana, Slovenia

E-mail: *tomaz.erzar@guest.arnes.si*

Katarina Kompan Erzar

Assistant Prof., Faculty of Theology, University of Ljubljana, Slovenia

Marcin Godawa

Dr. Hab., Assistant Prof.

The Pontifical University of John Paul II in Cracow

E-mail: *marcin2409@interia.pl*

Stanislav Slatinek

Assistant Prof., Faculty of Theology, University of Ljubljana, Slovenia

E-mail: *stanislav.slatinek@guest.arnes.si*

Tadej Strehovec

Assistant Prof., Faculty of Theology, University of Ljubljana, Slovenia

E-mail: *tadej.strehovec@teof.uni-lj.si*